MATTHEW
HENSON

# MATTHEW HENSON

*Michael Gilman*

Senior Consulting Editor
**Nathan Irvin Huggins**
Director
*W.E.B. Du Bois Institute for Afro-American Research*
*Harvard University*

CHELSEA HOUSE PUBLISHERS
*Philadelphia*

*Editor-in-Chief*   Nancy Toff
*Executive Editor*   Remmel T. Nunn
*Managing Editor*   Karyn Gullen Browne
*Copy Chief*   Juliann Barbato
*Picture Editor*   Adrian G. Allen
*Art Director*   Giannella Garrett
*Manufacturing Manager*   Gerald Levine

*Staff for* MATTHEW HENSON
*Senior Editor*   Richard Rennert
*Associate Editor*   Perry King
*Assistant Editor*   Gillian Bucky
*Copy Editor*   Terrance Dolan
*Editorial Assistant*   Laura-Ann Dolce
*Associate Picture Editor*   Juliette Dickstein
*Picture Researcher*   Faith Schornick
*Senior Designer*   Laurie Jewell
*Design Assistant*   Laura Lang
*Production Coordinator*   Joseph Romano
*Cover Illustration*   **Bradford Brown**

*Creative Director*   Harold Steinberg

15 14

Library of Congress Cataloging in Publication Data

Gilman, Michael.
   Matthew Henson.

   (Black Americans of achievement)
   Bibliography: p.
   Includes index.
   Summary: Follows the life of the black explorer who accom-
panied Robert Peary on the expedition to the North Pole.
   1. Henson, Matthew Alexander, 1866–1955—Juvenile lit-
erature.   2. Explorers—United States—Biography—Juvenile
literature.   3. North Pole—Juvenile literature. [1. Henson,
Matthew Alexander, 1866–1955.   2. Explorers.   3. Afro-
Americans—Biography]   I. Title.   II. Series.
G635.H4G55   1988      919.8′.04 [B] [92]      87-24253
ISBN 1-55546-590-0
      0-7910-0207-1   (pbk.)

# CONTENTS

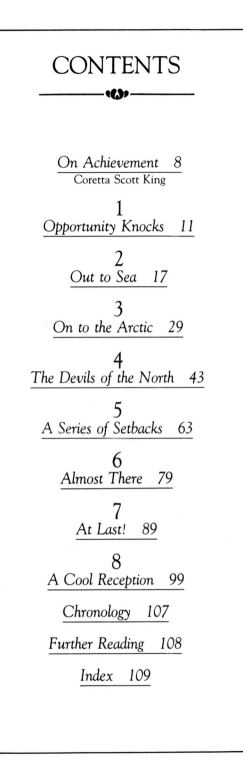

# BLACK AMERICANS OF ACHIEVEMENT

HENRY AARON
*baseball great*

KAREEM ABDUL-JABBAR
*basketball great*

MUHAMMAD ALI
*heavyweight champion*

RICHARD ALLEN
*religious leader and
social activist*

MAYA ANGELOU
*author*

LOUIS ARMSTRONG
*musician*

ARTHUR ASHE
*tennis great*

JOSEPHINE BAKER
*entertainer*

JAMES BALDWIN
*author*

BENJAMIN BANNEKER
*scientist and mathematician*

AMIRI BARAKA
*poet and playwright*

COUNT BASIE
*bandleader and composer*

ROMARE BEARDEN
*artist*

JAMES BECKWOURTH
*frontiersman*

MARY MCLEOD BETHUNE
*educator*

GEORGE WASHINGTON
CARVER
*botanist*

CHARLES CHESNUTT
*author*

BILL COSBY
*entertainer*

PAUL CUFFE
*merchant and abolitionist*

MILES DAVIS
*musician*

FATHER DIVINE
*religious leader*

FREDERICK DOUGLASS
*abolitionist editor*

CHARLES DREW
*physician*

W. E. B. DU BOIS
*scholar and activist*

PAUL LAURENCE DUNBAR
*poet*

DUKE ELLINGTON
*bandleader and composer*

RALPH ELLISON
*author*

JULIUS ERVING
*basketball great*

LOUIS FARRAKHAN
*political activist*

ELLA FITZGERALD
*singer*

MARCUS GARVEY
*black nationalist leader*

JOSH GIBSON
*baseball great*

WHOOPI GOLDBERG
*entertainer*

ALEX HALEY
*author*

PRINCE HALL
*social reformer*

JIMI HENDRIX
*musician*

MATTHEW HENSON
*explorer*

BILLIE HOLIDAY
*singer*

LENA HORNE
*entertainer*

WHITNEY HOUSTON
*singer and actress*

LANGSTON HUGHES
*poet*

ZORA NEALE HURSTON
*author*

JESSE JACKSON
*civil-rights leader and politician*

MICHAEL JACKSON
*entertainer*

JACK JOHNSON
*heavyweight champion*

MAGIC JOHNSON
*basketball great*

SCOTT JOPLIN
*composer*

BARBARA JORDAN
*politician*

MICHAEL JORDAN
*basketball great*

CORETTA SCOTT KING
*civil-rights leader*

MARTIN LUTHER KING, JR.
*civil-rights leader*

LEWIS LATIMER
*scientist*

SPIKE LEE
*filmmaker*

CARL LEWIS
*champion athlete*

JOE LOUIS
*heavyweight champion*

RONALD MCNAIR
*astronaut*

MALCOLM X
*militant black leader*

BOB MARLEY
*musician*

THURGOOD MARSHALL
*Supreme Court justice*

TONI MORRISON
*author*

ELIJAH MUHAMMAD
*religious leader*

EDDIE MURPHY
*entertainer*

JESSE OWENS
*champion athlete*

SATCHEL PAIGE
*baseball great*

CHARLIE PARKER
*musician*

ROSA PARKS
*civil-rights leader*

COLIN POWELL
*military leader*

PAUL ROBESON
*singer and actor*

JACKIE ROBINSON
*baseball great*

DIANA ROSS
*entertainer*

WILL SMITH
*actor*

CLARENCE THOMAS
*Supreme Court justice*

SOJOURNER TRUTH
*antislavery activist*

HARRIET TUBMAN
*antislavery activist*

NAT TURNER
*slave revolt leader*

DENMARK VESEY
*slave revolt leader*

ALICE WALKER
*author*

MADAM C. J. WALKER
*entrepreneur*

BOOKER T. WASHINGTON
*educator*

DENZEL WASHINGTON
*actor*

OPRAH WINFREY
*entertainer*

TIGER WOODS
*golf star*

RICHARD WRIGHT
*author*

# ON
# ACHIEVEMENT

—————— ✧ ——————

*Coretta Scott King*

BEFORE YOU BEGIN this book, I hope you will ask yourself what the word excellence means to you. I think that it's a question we should all ask, and keep asking as we grow older and change. Because the truest answer to it should never change. When you think of excellence, perhaps you think of success at work; or of becoming wealthy; or meeting the right person, getting married, and having a good family life.

Those important goals are worth striving for, but there is a better way to look at excellence. As Martin Luther King, Jr., said in one of his last sermons, "I want you to be first in love. I want you to be first in moral excellence. I want you to be first in generosity. If you want to be important, wonderful. If you want to be great, wonderful. But recognize that he who is greatest among you shall be your servant."

My husband, Martin Luther King, Jr., knew that the true meaning of achievement is service. When I met him, in 1952, he was already ordained as a Baptist preacher and was working towards a doctoral degree at Boston University. I was studying at the New England Conservatory and dreamed of accomplishments in music. We married a year later, and after I graduated the following year we moved to Montgomery, Alabama. We didn't know it then, but our notions of achievement were about to undergo a dramatic change.

You may have read or heard about what happened next. What began with the boycott of a local bus line grew into a national movement, and by the time he was assassinated in 1968 my husband had fashioned a black movement powerful enough to shatter forever the practice of racial segregation. What you may not have read about is where he got his method for resisting injustice without compromising his religious beliefs.

He got the strategy of nonviolence from a man of a different race, who lived in a distant country, and even practiced a different religion. The man was Mahatma Gandhi, the great leader of India, who devoted his life to serving humanity in the spirit of love and nonviolence. It was in these principles that Martin discovered his method for social reform. More than anything else, those two principles were the key to his achievements.

This book is about black Americans who served society through the excellence of their achievements. It forms a part of the rich history of black men and women in America—a history of stunning accomplishments in every field of human endeavor, from literature and art to science, industry, education, diplomacy, athletics, jurisprudence, even polar exploration.

Not all of the people in this history had the same ideals, but I think you will find something that all of them have in common. Like Martin Luther King, Jr., they all decided to become "drum majors" and serve humanity. In that principle—whether it was expressed in books, inventions, or song—they found something outside themselves to use as a goal and a guide. Something that showed them a way to serve others, instead of living only for themselves.

Reading the stories of these courageous men and women not only helps us discover the principles that we will use to guide our own lives, but it teaches us about our black heritage and about America itself. It is crucial for us to know the heroes and heroines of our history and to realize that the price we paid in our struggle for equality in America was dear. But we must also understand that we have gotten as far as we have partly because America's democratic system and ideals made it possible.

We still are struggling with racism and prejudice. But the great men and women in this series are a tribute to the spirit of our democratic ideals and the system in which they have flourished. And that makes their stories special, and worth knowing. ✤

# 1

## OPPORTUNITY KNOCKS

ON A SPRING DAY in 1887, Lieutenant Robert E. Peary of the U.S. Navy Civil Engineer Corps hurried down G Street in Washington, D.C. Working on an assignment for the Maritime Canal Company, the 31-year-old naval officer was about to lead a surveying expedition to Nicaragua, where he hoped to discover a suitable route through the Central American jungle for a proposed waterway to link the Atlantic and Pacific oceans. Preparations for the excursion to Nicaragua were well under way, and Peary himself had been charged with outfitting the expedition. With this in mind, he slowed his gait and stopped in front of B. H. Steinmetz and Sons, hatters.

Peary entered the shop, nodded a curt hello to Steinmetz, and indicated that he was in need of a sun helmet, size seven and three-eighths. Steinmetz turned and called Peary's order to the back room. While the two men waited for the order to be filled, Peary began to talk about his upcoming trip. Then, remembering that the Maritime Canal Company had said it would pay for a servant to accompany him on the expedition, he asked Steinmetz if he could recommend a young man for the position.

The store owner thought for a moment. He then said that his stock clerk, Matthew Henson, might be

*In 1887, Matthew Henson and Robert Peary, who would eventually reach the North Pole together, first met in the Washington, D.C., hat store where Henson was employed. This view of Pennsylvania Avenue shows the capital during that period.*

MATTHEW A. HENSON

*When Henson was a young man, he hoped to lead a life of adventure and become famous. However, he probably never dreamed that one day his face would appear on souvenir cards that were given away with cigarette packs.*

interested in the job. Although Henson had been working in the shop for the past 18 months, it was known that he wanted to travel. He was a reliable and hard worker, Steinmetz assured Peary. And he learned quickly.

Just then, the young black man entered from the back room, carrying a hatbox which he set on the counter in front of Peary.

Although Henson was only 20 years old, he had already traveled throughout much of the world. Beginning at the age of 13, he had visited almost every major seaport, first as a cabin boy and later as a trained seaman. His early years at sea had fueled his passion for adventure, and he aspired to a life of excitement. But when he returned to the United States, his hopes had been crushed. Opportunities for advancement were severely limited for blacks in the United States at the turn of the century.

Accordingly, Henson was forced to take a series of menial jobs to support himself. Having experienced a great deal of racial prejudice in the past, he despaired of ever finding an outlet to satisfy his desires. With his life at a standstill, he had taken the job as a stock clerk in the hat shop. Yet he still hoped that an opportunity to travel would materialize.

The man whose hat Henson carried to the counter shared many of the young stock clerk's enthusiasms. Born in 1856, Peary had grown up in Maine and had been something of a loner from an early age. Not a very sociable person, he prided himself on his resourcefulness and his skill at hunting and fishing. After graduating from Bowdoin College in Maine with a degree in civil engineering, he started a surveying business, which soon failed.

During his first few years out of school, Peary found few opportunities to satisfy his longing for adventure. After a while, he moved to Washington,

D.C., and took a job as a draftsman for the U.S. Coast and Geodetic Survey. At that time, many members of Congress and the business community were discussing the possibility of building an inter-ocean canal through Central America. Peary was taken with the idea. Already bored with his new job, he thought that tropical canal explorations might provide him with the adventure he was seeking. In 1880, he wrote to his mother about his aspirations: "I don't want to live and die without accomplishing anything or without being known beyond a narrow circle of friends." He was determined to become a famous explorer.

In 1881, Peary took the entrance examination for the Civil Engineer Corps of the U.S. Navy. He was selected for the corps and given the rank of lieutenant. After quickly proving his ability, he was sent to Nicaragua to look for a possible canal route.

On the way to Nicaragua, Peary stumbled upon an idea that would eclipse his tropical aspirations and obsess his thoughts for almost 30 years. Only one accomplishment, he realized, could bring him fame equal to that of the person whom he considered to be the greatest explorer: Christopher Columbus. That accomplishment was to reach the North Pole.

Many others before Peary had attempted to penetrate the polar region. Arctic exploration had been taking place since the time of the ancient Greeks, as men throughout history attempted to decipher the mystery of what lay at the top of the world. By the late 19th century, knowledge about the Arctic and the North Pole was still limited. However, the most recent explorations had finally disproved the centuries-old belief that the North Pole lay at the heart of an open arctic sea encircled by a ring of ice.

Most of the earliest excursions to the Arctic had been motivated by commercial interests. In searching

A lieutenant in the U.S. Navy Civil Engineer Corps, Robert Peary was preparing to lead a surveying expedition to Nicaragua when he met Henson, a clerk at the B. H. Steinmetz and Sons hat store.

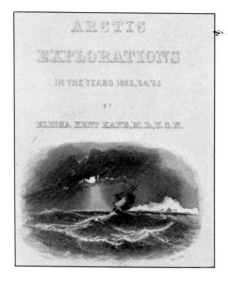

*The American explorer Elisha Kent Kane was one of the first men to make a serious attempt to reach the North Pole. In the 1850s, he led an expedition to the northwestern coast of Greenland.*

for an economical trade route from Europe to the Far East that would take them across the top of the world, countless men risked their lives. However, these explorers failed to find such a northwest passage. Consequently, by the mid-19th century, arctic exploration had turned into a search for the North Pole itself. This search soon became a race fueled by nationalistic pride, the desire for adventure, and the egos of men like Peary.

In 1885, after completing his survey of Nicaragua, Peary returned to Washington, D.C. Although he resumed working full-time for the navy, his obsession with the North Pole had grown. He spent all of his spare time researching the polar region and the ice caps of Greenland, where he believed lay the key to the mysteries of the Pole.

In 1886, Peary was granted six months' leave by the navy. He promptly voyaged north to Greenland and returned home elated, hoping to arrange a second trip. However, the navy ordered him back to Nicaragua to resume work on the canal. He was to command the entire expedition this time.

And so, in the spring of 1887, his dream of arctic exploration postponed indefinitely, a resigned Peary found himself in a hat store in the nation's capital, about to embark for the tropics.

As Peary tried on the sun helmet, he studied Henson, noting the young man's compact, sturdy build and pleasant, honest face. Peary then introduced himself and explained his situation, telling Henson that Steinmetz had highly recommended the young man for the job of Peary's servant. In Nicaragua, the living conditions would be primitive, Peary added. The climate was hot and humid. There would not be any time off, and the work would be grueling. But it would give the young clerk a chance to be part of a history-making venture.

Henson gave Peary's proposal a moment's thought before saying, "Sir, I'd like the job very much."

The expedition to Nicaragua was just the first of many exciting adventures that Peary and Henson would experience together. ✺

*Like these three fur-clad explorers, Henson eventually became a veteran of the Far North. However, his first expedition with Peary took him to the rain forests of Central America.*

# 2

# OUT
# TO SEA

MATTHEW ALEXANDER HENSON was born on August 8, 1866, on his parents' farm near the Potomac River in Charles County, Maryland. A little more than a year before his birth, the North's triumph in the Civil War had helped to bring about an end to slavery in the United States. Matthew's parents had spent their entire lives as free blacks in the South, where the majority of blacks were slaves. Therefore, their situation was not changed by Congress's passage of the Thirteenth Amendment to the Constitution, which granted liberty to all American slaves in 1865.

Along with many former slaves, Matthew's parents were subjected to attacks by the Ku Klux Klan and other white supremacist groups that terrorized southern blacks after the Civil War. Seeking to stop blacks from exercising their newly won rights to vote and to attend public schools, gangs of white-robed Klansmen descended on the homes of black families at night, leaving burning crosses as reminders of their visits. Blacks were sometimes kidnapped and lynched by white mobs. To escape from this racial violence, the Hensons sold their small Maryland farm in 1867 and moved to a poor section in Georgetown, on the outskirts of Washington, D.C.

*Orphaned when he was 13 years old, Henson went to sea as a cabin boy on a merchant ship.*

June 28; 1882.                    Chapel Point.  Port Tobacco Creek, Charles Co. Md.

*Born in August 1866, 16 months after the end of the Civil War, Henson spent his first year on a small farm near this one in Charles County, Maryland.*

Matthew's mother died when Matthew was seven years old. His father subsequently sent him to stay with an uncle who lived nearby. He attended a black public school for the next six years, during the last of which he took a summer job washing dishes in a restaurant.

Matthew's early years were marked by one especially memorable event. When he was 10 years old, he went to a ceremony honoring Abraham Lincoln, the American president who had fought so hard to preserve the Union during the Civil War and had issued the proclamation that had freed slaves in the Confederate states in 1863. At the ceremony, Matthew was greatly inspired by a speech given by Frederick Douglass, the longtime leading figure in the American black community. A former slave turned abolitionist, Douglass called upon blacks to vigorously pursue educational opportunities and battle racial prejudice.

By the time Matthew turned 13 years old, his father had died and his uncle found that he could no longer care for Matthew. To support himself, he became a waiter and dishwasher at the restaurant at which he had previously worked during the summers. The restaurant's owner, a kind woman whom everyone called Aunt Jenny, let Matthew sleep in the kitchen and eat leftover food. But he soon grew restless waiting on tables. He wanted adventure.

One of the regulars at Aunt Jenny's restaurant was an old sailor named Baltimore Jack who liked to talk about life on the seas. Matthew listened to the sailor's stories and decided that working on a ship would be exciting. Instead of returning to school in the fall of 1879, he set out for the port of Baltimore, Maryland.

After walking 40 miles to Baltimore, Matthew went down to the harbor to look for a ship that needed a cabin boy. At the end of one pier was anchored a

*Frightened by the attacks of the violent white-supremacist group, the Ku Klux Klan, Henson's parents sold their farm in 1867 and moved to Washington, D.C.*

ship called the *Katie Hines,* and by the ship was standing its silver-haired, full-bearded captain. Introducing himself to the man, Matthew explained his situation and asked if he could join the ship. The captain was so impressed with the boy's self-assured manner that he agreed to take him on board. Matthew would perform all of the tasks usually given to a ship's cabin boy, from peeling potatoes in the ship's mess to mopping down the decks.

For the next five years, Matthew sailed with Captain Childs and the *Katie Hines* to ports in China, Japan, Africa, France, the Russian Arctic seas, and many other areas. The captain took a special interest in his cabin boy's education and used history and geography books to give Matthew reading and writing lessons. Matthew also received training in carpentry, ship's mechanics, first aid, and other practical subjects, and he gradually became a trained seaman.

An unpleasant incident during Matthew's first months on the *Katie Hines* almost destroyed his desire to become a skilled sailor. One day, when he was alone in the ship's mess, a bigoted white seaman named Frenchy insulted him and beat him up. Feeling worthless and humiliated, Matthew lost all interest in learning. He decided that to people like Frenchy he would always be a "goddamned nigger," no matter how great his accomplishments. At first, Captain Childs scolded him about his lack of effort. But when Matthew explained to the captain about the fight and its effect on him, Childs persuaded him he must fight to overcome ignorance and prejudice. The captain assured him that by using his knowledge and intelligence, he could make people respect him.

By the time Henson was 18 years old, he had become a valued member of the *Katie Hines*'s crew. In December 1883, Captain Childs became sick while the ship was sailing from Jamaica to Baltimore. He soon died and was buried at sea.

No longer feeling at home on the *Katie Hines*, Henson signed on with a ship called the *White Seal*, which went on a seal-hunting voyage off Newfoundland, Canada, in the north Atlantic. Disgusted by the ship's drunken captain and its undisciplined and bigoted crew, he left the *White Seal* when it docked in Saint John's, Newfoundland. Finding another ship on which the crew did not treat black sailors badly proved to be very difficult.

During the next three years, Henson traveled around the eastern United States, staying for a while in various places to earn money. He worked as a night watchman, a dockworker, a chauffeur, a messenger

*Members of the racially integrated crew of a U.S. Navy ship pose for a picture. After Henson joined the merchant ship* Katie Hines, *he visited ports around the world and became a trained seaman.*

*Like these desperate people picking through a garbage heap in front of the Capitol building in Washington, D.C., Henson had to struggle to survive. Good work opportunities for black Americans in the late 1800s were limited.*

boy, and a bellhop. He eventually returned to Washington, D.C., and took a job as a clerk in Steinmetz's hat store, where he was offered the opportunity to become Lieutenant Robert Peary's servant.

Although Henson was hesitant about taking a job as a servant, Peary's expedition to Nicaragua seemed to offer the adventure that Henson so desired. Peary's expedition in 1887 to find a route for a canal from the Atlantic to the Pacific Ocean took place when ships still had to sail around the southern tip of South America to get from one ocean to the other. A French company had already begun to dig a canal in Panama (which at that time was part of Colombia), but progress was slow because of the project's financial problems and the effects of malaria and other tropical diseases on the work force. It was beginning to look as though the canal might never be finished. Consequently, the American-based Maritime Canal Company began to investigate the possibility of making a separate attempt. The company enlisted the help of the U.S. Navy in searching for a more viable route for a canal in Nicaragua, about 350 miles up the coast from the French project in Panama. Peary had done preliminary work there in 1884 and 1885.

The 170-mile course that Peary was to survey ran through swampy and heavily forested areas. He brought with him a group of 45 engineers and surveyors and 100 black laborers from Jamaica. The expedition force was divided into six teams, and the laborers' job was to hack a path through the jungle while the engineers made their measurements of the terrain and drew maps. Peary's duties required him to travel between the teams, each of which worked on different sections of the route. As Peary's servant, Henson had to make sure that Peary had clean clothes when he returned to camp.

*While Lieutenant Robert Peary led an American expedition to Nicaragua in 1887 in search of a route for a canal that would link the Atlantic and Pacific oceans, a French company was already digging a canal in Panama (shown here).*

*Working in the treacherous swamps of the Nicaraguan jungle, Henson proved to be an invaluable addition to Peary's expedition and was promoted from servant to chainman on a surveying team.*

Henson's first task when he got to Nicaragua was to build a headquarters for Peary. Using plans that the lieutenant had drawn up, Henson directed a squad of laborers to complete the building. Peary returned from his initial checks on the surveying crews to discover that Henson had added many useful features to the structure.

The surveying work progressed. Every day, the workers struggled to slash their way through the forests with their machetes. They often found themselves running into the bases of hills that had been hidden by the trees. At other times, they had to wade through waist-deep water while being attacked by swarms of insects.

Henson's duties as a servant were limited, and he wanted more challenging work than just cleaning the mud off Peary's uniforms. The Nicaraguan jungle, which most of the expedition's members found unbearable, soon provided Henson with his opportunity for new employment. One day, a member of one of the surveying crews was brought into camp after having been pulled out of quicksand. The man, who had sunk in the quicksand up to his chest, had been so frightened by his experience that he quit his job as a chainman—the person who holds the chain along which a surveyor makes his measurements. When Henson heard that there was an opening on the surveying team, he told Peary he wanted the job. Because no one else wanted the chainman's job, Peary agreed to let Henson try it.

The job of chainman on a surveying crew requires a steady hand and enormous patience. Working in the oppressive jungle environment, Henson had to hold one end of a chain perfectly straight while the surveyor sighted along the chain from the other end. Even the smallest movements by Henson could ruin a measurement. He could not change his grip on the chain or even brush away the insects that were biting him.

Henson did his job very well, and he earned strong praise from his supervisor on the surveying crew. Accordingly, he never worked as a servant again. Before long, he was promoted to the position of Peary's personal chainman, and he helped the lieutenant check on the measurements made by his surveying crews.

For nearly a half year, Peary and Henson traveled together, enduring extreme heat and torrential rainstorms. Henson continued to acquire useful skills, and he soon became an expert at shooting a rifle and handling a canoe. Although Peary treated Henson fairly, the lieutenant had an aloof manner and shared no confidences with his chainman. However, Henson, who had learned that Peary was hoping to lead an expedition to unexplored areas in the Far North, began to feel that it would be worthwhile to stay with the reserved, hard-driving naval officer.

*During the return voyage from Nicaragua in 1888, Peary invited Henson to join him in an expedition to the Arctic. Icebergs such as this one were just one of the obstacles they would face.*

The surveying crews finished their work in June 1888. Sailing home, Henson was proud of the good work he had done and of the new skills he had mastered. Yet he also felt let down. He worried that he would never again have the chance to explore new parts of the world or to use the knowledge and talents he had acquired. There were few good opportunities for blacks in the United States, and he feared that he would have to take a dull job that offered him little hope of gaining any distinction.

A few days before the ship reached New York, Peary called Henson into his cabin. The lieutenant was in a somewhat excited state, and he began the conversation by thanking Henson for his good work—this was indeed a special occasion, for it was the first direct praise that the lieutenant had ever given Henson. Peary then told him about his hopes of exploring the world's north polar regions. At that time, no man had ever gotten within 600 miles of the North Pole. Peary said that it was his mission to map the unexplored areas of the Arctic. He believed that much scientifically valuable information could be discovered about the weather, ocean currents, and animal life in the polar regions.

Continuing his discussion of the Arctic, Peary told Henson about his first trip to Greenland two years before. He planned on returning to the Arctic as soon as he could raise the money for another expedition and obtain a leave of absence from the navy. All the while, Henson grew excited by Peary's talk about a new adventure.

After the lieutenant finished explaining about the upcoming expedition, he asked Henson if he wanted to be part of it. Life in the polar wastelands, Peary told him, could be difficult for a "son of the equator." This remark cemented Henson's decision. When he was a member of the *Katie Hines*, he had spent part of a winter in the port of Murmansk in northern

Russia, and he knew that he could withstand the rigors of an extremely cold climate. He quickly agreed to join Peary on his trip to Greenland.

Welcoming Henson to the expedition, Peary then explained with embarrassment that he could not afford to pay anything to the men who signed on with him. Henson laughed. He doubted that money would be of much use in the Far North, he said. Peary nodded at this answer, realizing that in Henson he had found a man who shared his own desire to test himself in unknown regions and who would endure great hardships to win a name for himself. The lure of the North was calling both of them. ✺

*Having spent part of a winter in northern Russia when he was a sailor, Henson had no doubts that he could survive in the Far North—but he also knew the dangers. This trapped ship is being crushed by the ice.*

# 3

# ON TO
# THE ARCTIC

AFTER THE NICARAGUA surveying expedition returned to the United States in 1888, Henson worked at various odd jobs while waiting for Peary to make the preparations for their trip to Greenland. Because arctic exploration was an expensive occupation, Peary had to win the financial support of many organizations and wealthy individuals to carry out his plans. He also had naval duties to fulfill, and soon after returning to the United States, he was assigned to supervise construction work at the Brooklyn naval yards. In 1889, his plans for the voyage north were pushed back still further when he married Josephine, his longtime sweetheart.

A year later, Peary was assigned to work at the naval yards in Philadelphia, Pennsylvania. Yet he was still caught up in planning his expedition. While finding a messenger's job for Henson at the naval yards, he gave lectures about arctic exploration to stir up interest in his project. Peary was eventually able to obtain financial support from three scientific organizations. Contributions were also solicited from men who applied to join Peary's expedition.

Henson was already well aware of the hazards of traveling in the Arctic from his conversations with Peary and from his own reading about previous ex-

*Crunching its way through drifting ice floes, a ship moves slowly ahead. Outfitting an expedition to go to the Arctic was an expensive business and required financial backing from scientific organizations and wealthy patrons.*

*Henson stands in front of the huge wheel of a ship. During 1890 and early 1891, he worked as a messenger at the Philadelphia naval yards and helped Peary make preparations for their first trip to the Arctic.*

peditions. A few years before, a U.S. Army expedition to Greenland led by Lieutenant Adolphus Greely had set a record for the highest northern latitude reached by man, but most of the group's members died during the attempt. Although Henson knew that many people believed he was crazy to want to go to the Far North, he was nonetheless surprised and angered when one of the officers at the navy yards told him that black men could not survive in the arctic regions. The man said that he would bet $100 that Henson would not return with his fingers and toes intact. The officer believed that Henson would be a victim of frostbite, a condition that occurs when parts of the body such as the ears, nose, fingers, and toes are not protected adequately from the cold and thus become frozen. The only way to stop the effects of severe frostbite is amputation. Henson vowed that he would be careful, and he accepted the man's bet.

Peary had promised Henson that he would have to do the work of three men on the expedition. While preparations for the trip were being made in Philadelphia in 1891, Henson was kept busy helping the lieutenant assemble the supplies he would need. His enthusiasm grew stronger as he met the other men who would be sailing with him. The other expedition members included Eivand Astrup, a Norwegian who was an expert in cross-country skiing; Frederick Cook, a medical doctor who wished to study the life of the native Greenlanders, the Eskimos; Langdon Gibson, a hunter who also studied birds; and John Verhoeff, a wealthy young man who was an amateur geologist. Filling out the group was Peary's young bride, Josephine. A team of scientists from the Philadelphia Academy of Natural Sciences was also coming along, although it would not remain in Greenland. The scientists would return to the United States with the ship that Peary had chartered to take them north.

Each expedition member signed an agreement stating that he would obey Peary's orders and would not write or speak in public about their experiences until one year after the commander had done so. This restriction gave Peary the freedom to lecture and raise funds for future trips without any competition from other expedition members. Peary managed to find $50 in his budget for Henson, but all of the other men were unpaid volunteers.

On June 6, 1891, Henson began his first voyage to the Arctic. Peary's expedition sailed from Brooklyn, New York, on the *Kite*, a ship that had made many seal-hunting voyages in the northern seas. Henson immediately became busy securing up the ship's leaky joints, and he also performed cooking and carpentry work. During one bad storm, rough seas damaged the tiny *Kite*, and it began to take on water. Henson and Peary helped the ship's crew work the pumps until the danger was over.

Shortly after the voyage began, the team members met in Peary's cabin to hear him lecture about the geography and climate of Greenland. The commander described how thousands of square miles of land lay buried beneath an ice cap that was a mile thick in some places. Beneath these massive glaciers, whole mountains were locked in ice. At the coast, the landscape showed in great, jagged relief. The interior mountain ranges extended to the sea in many areas, and the shoreline was cut by many steep-sided bays called fjords, which were worn into the rocky coasts by the grinding power of glacial ice. The seas around much of the northern half of Greenland were iced over throughout the year, making travel there by ship impossible. Speculating that Greenland's ice cap might extend all the way to the North Pole, Peary was planning to map the land's unexplored northern coast.

On June 23, 1891, the *Kite* sailed into Baffin Bay, off Greenland's western coast, and Henson got his first glimpse of the land where he would be living for the next 14 months. Huge sheets of ice called ice

*In the early 1800s, Lieutenant Adolphus Greely (shown here) led an expedition to the Arctic that set a record for the farthest north latitude reached by man. However, 16 of the team's 23 members died in the attempt.*

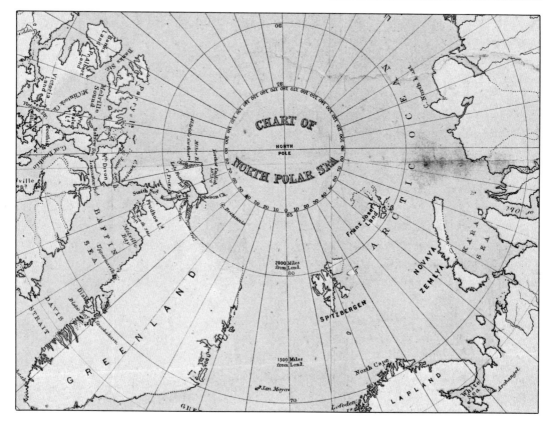

On this map of the north polar regions, which was made during the 1880s, the unexplored coast of northern Greenland is left blank. Peary planned to travel to this region during the first expedition he commanded in the Arctic.

floes were floating in the bay, and the tough little *Kite* had to ram its way between them to continue the voyage northward. A few days before the ship reached its destination, an ice floe hit the *Kite*'s rudder, the flat steering board that projects below the ship. The collision caused the tiller, which is connected to the rudder, to break free.

Peary, who was standing nearby, was struck by the tiller, and the bones in the lower part of his right leg were broken. He was carried to his cabin, where Dr. Cook set the bones and placed a cast on the broken leg. Peary's companions thought that the expedition was finished, but the commander, showing his strength of character, which Henson had seen him display in Nicaragua, insisted that everything would continue as planned. A few days later, the ship reached its destination in McCormick Bay, an inlet on the northwestern coast of Greenland. Peary had himself carried ashore on planks, and before long he was moving around on a pair of crutches that Henson had made for him.

Crutches were but one of the many things that Henson had to build. Peary had not exaggerated when he told Henson that he would be required to do the work of three men. First, he constructed the team's house, a building made of stones, sod, canvas, and tar paper that measured 21 feet by 12 feet. The house had two rooms: one for Peary and his wife and one for Henson and the other four team members. The commander had designed the building to withstand the extreme cold of Greenland's winters, and he named it Red Cliff House after a nearby lichen-covered slope. With the other team members pursuing their studies and Peary on crutches, Henson did all of the construction by himself. Luckily, it was summertime, and the temperatures were fairly moderate, reaching between 40°F and 50°F.

At the end of July, the *Kite* sailed away, leaving the expedition without any hope of receiving supplies until the following summer, for sheets of ice began to spread across the northern areas of Baffin Bay, sealing it off from ships. After finishing Red Cliff House, Henson's next job was to make sledges, the large sleds upon which supplies would be hauled on the trip across Greenland's ice cap. The sledges' heavy oak pieces could not be nailed or bolted together because metal could become brittle and crack in the Arctic's subzero temperatures. Therefore, Henson had to drill dozens of holes in the hard wood, through which he inserted strips of walrus hide to hold the sledge together.

Henson soon discovered that being black could be a distinct advantage in the Arctic. At the invitation of the expedition members, an Eskimo family

*Although Peary's leg was broken in an accident on the ship during the voyage to Greenland in 1891, he resolutely insisted that the expedition must continue as planned.*

*An Eskimo family shares a joke at dinner. Mistaking the dark-skinned Henson for a long-lost member of their tribe, the Eskimos adopted him into their community*

that had been traveling in the area came to stay near their camp. One of the Eskimos, a man named Ikwah, spotted Henson and ran over to him, speaking excitedly in the Eskimo language. The man held his arm next to Henson's for comparison, and Henson saw that their skin color was similar. Ikwah grinned and said, "Innuit, Innuit," repeating the Eskimo word for his people. Because Henson was not a *kabloona* (a white person), Ikwah believed that Henson must be an Eskimo who had become lost from his tribe and had forgotten his true language.

Ikwah and his family decided to adopt Henson. However, Ikwah refused to learn any English words until Henson learned how to speak Eskimo, so Henson quickly began to master the language. His ability to communicate with the local peoples and his strong friendship with them would be of immense value during his years in the North.

Word spread fast among the Eskimos in the region that at Peary's camp they could obtain fine goods such as knives and tobacco in exchange for their animal skins and meat. Before long, several more families decided to settle at McCormick Bay for the winter. As the days grew shorter and colder, the Eskimos began to build the domed ice and snow shelters they called igloos. Peary was glad that the Eskimos were attracted to his camp because he needed to buy dog teams from them to pull his sledges in the spring.

In the Far North, it is light for almost 24 hours each day in June and July. By September, however, daytime light is reduced to a dim, brief twilight. Then the sun virtually disappears—except for a faint glow on the southern horizon—until February. For two weeks during the winter months, traveling or hunting is possible only by moonlight—if the skies are clear.

*Supplies being transported by dog teams pulling sledges over the arctic ice. Through the patient instructions of his Eskimo friends, Henson became the most skilled driver in Peary's team.*

The arctic winter's endless nights were extremely wearying on some of the expedition members. With the exception of Peary and Henson, the men in the team found the small house difficult to live in and constantly got on each other's nerves. Some of the men developed a strong resentment toward the Pearys, who had a room to themselves. They especially became angry at Josephine Peary, who insisted that the men dress up for dinner. Nevertheless, they were able to practice using their skis and snowshoes to relieve their boredom.

With his broken leg mending quickly, Peary busied himself with his plans for the next spring's journey north. And thanks to his adoption by the Eskimos, Henson also adapted well to the long frozen nights. Ikwah and another Eskimo man, Ahnalka, took him on long hunting trips, teaching him how to track and kill caribou, polar bears, seals, walruses, and musk oxen. He often stayed as a guest in the igloos of his Eskimo friends, and he not only learned their language but also participated in their work and games. They called Henson "Miy Paluk" (kind little Matthew) and served him special foods, such as whole birds pickled in seal oil. Often treated to Eskimo

*One of Henson's first tasks after the expedition landed at Mc-Cormick Bay was to build the sledges (including the one shown here) that would be used to haul supplies over Greenland's ice cap.*

entertainments, during which his hosts would dance and sing while beating on drums, Henson in turn pulled out an accordion and sang hymns that he had learned when he was a boy. His hosts were amazed and delighted by the strange new sounds.

One of the most important skills that Henson learned from the Eskimos was the handling of a sledge and dog team. A typical sledge was pulled by 8 powerful dogs, each of which was harnessed to a 15-foot-long leather line known as a trace. All the traces were connected to a controlling device known as a toggle, which the driver held in one hand. In his other hand, the driver held a long whip, which he snapped over the dog's heads to urge them on. When pulling the sledge, the dog team spread out in front in a fan shape.

Henson spent many hours trying to learn how to snap his whip just above the ear of the dog he wanted to command. But if he failed to yell the proper word as the whip snapped, the dogs would not move. Again and again, his errant whip sprayed snow on the bewildered dogs or caught them on the back, head, or rump, causing them to stop and snarl at him. Sometimes he wrapped the whip around Ikwah or Ahnalka

by mistake and pulled them head over heels into the snow. They would lie there, laughing uncontrollably while the dogs sat, unmoving.

When Henson finally did get his dog team going, he had to run along behind the sledge, guiding the team with the whip and his voice. He steered by pushing on the handgrips that were connected to the driver's end of the sledge. It is a great tribute to Henson's ability to master new skills that in time he became a better driver than all but the most skillful Eskimo hunters.

After Henson learned how to drive a sledge, Peary came to him for lessons. The commander encountered the same difficulties that Henson had faced, but he was much less patient. During his first lesson, Peary began to curse his dogs when they would not move. Henson politely tried to conceal his amusement and, continuing his instructions, told Peary the words he should use when he wanted the dogs to stop. The commander responded by saying that if he got the dogs moving, he did not care if they stopped. In time, however, Peary became a competent driver. The other expedition members also learned how to drive a sledge, though they never became very proficient at it.

In the spring of 1892, as the daylight hours began to grow longer, Peary's team moved a ton of supplies onto the ice cap. At different points along the first part of the route that Peary intended to follow, supplies of food known as caches were stored and marked with a pole. With forward caches established, the expedition members could travel far inland knowing that they would have supplies to fall back upon.

The men worked in teams of two. They traveled one day's march apart, with Henson and Peary bringing up the rear. The men had to be careful when traveling around crevasses—the long, jagged openings in the ice field that could swallow a dog team in an instant. Two days into Henson and Peary's trek,

a snowstorm pinned them down. Neither of the two men knew how to build an igloo that would provide them with shelter from the freezing winds, and they were forced to huddle in sleeping bags until the storm ended. The intense cold froze Henson's left eye, causing damage to the cornea that would continue to bother him for months to come. Two days after their ordeal, Henson and Peary were finally able to join the rest of the teams.

After reaching the point where the most recent cache was established, Peary decided that two men could travel more efficiently than the whole group. He and Astrup, the expert skier, journeyed onward across the ice cap, while Henson and the others were instructed to return to Red Cliff House.

During the next three months, Henson served as a companion to Josephine Peary. The commander's wife grew ever more anxious as the weeks passed and Peary and Astrup failed to return. The Eskimos told

*An engraving shows the camp at Red Cliff House in the summer. As the daylight hours grew longer in the spring of 1892, Peary's team began to make caches of supplies on Greenland's ice cap.*

Henson they were glad that he had not gone out onto the ice cap, for a great devil named Kokoyah jealously guarded the area and killed anyone who went there. They were sure that Peary's party would never come back.

While waiting for Peary to return, Henson went hunting with the Eskimos. On one of the hunts, he killed his first polar bear. He estimated that the bear weighed more than 800 pounds, and he shuddered at the thought of what a blow from one of its giant paws could do to a man. He had already experienced a dangerous moment while hunting. On a hunting trip for walruses, he and some other team members had nearly had their boat overturned by a herd of the angry tusked animals.

On July 24, 1892, the *Kite* returned to pick up the expedition members. The ship needed to sail home within a few weeks in order to avoid being locked in the ice. Everyone began to share Josephine Peary's growing concern about her husband. On August 5, just as a search party led by Henson set out

*When Peary and Eivand Astrup finally returned on August 5, 1892, from their trek to the north coast of Greenland, they were met by a relief team led by Henson.*

to follow Peary's route, two men were spotted out on the ice cap. Peary and Astrup had finally returned.

The two men were thin and exhausted, and most of the dogs they had taken with them had died. Yet they were now jubilant. They had traveled 1,200 miles and discovered a new body of water—which Peary had named Independence Bay—off Greenland's previously unexplored northeast coast. Peary had already decided that he was going to return to Greenland with another expedition and conduct further explorations so that he could determine once and for all whether Greenland was an island or a land mass that extended to the North Pole. Even though Henson had not been on the trek to Independence Bay, he felt good about the skills he had learned on his first northern expedition. He told Peary that he, too, was eager to return.

The final days of the triumphant expedition were marred by tragedy. Young John Verhoeff went off on his own to collect some rock specimens, and days passed by without his return. Henson and a group of Eskimos eventually formed a search party and followed Verhoeff's trail, which ended at the edge of a gaping crevasse on the ice cap. They never found his body. "Kokoyah, eat kabloona," said Ikwah, who felt sure the angry devil had shown his displeasure at the invasion of his territory by Peary and Astrup by making a meal of Verhoeff.

The team members were all sobered by Verhoeff's death. Peary blamed himself for allowing Verhoeff to wander off alone. However, he was not going to let guilt or fear of personal injury deter him from further exploration. He told Henson that they were coming back and that they were going to find "the greatest prize since the discovery of the New World, the North Pole." These words echoed Henson's own feelings. He, too, had become committed to reaching the North Pole. ❧

# 4

# THE DEVILS
# OF THE NORTH

A TUMULTUOUS RECEPTION was awaiting the expedition members when the *Kite* docked in New York in September 1892. Americans hailed Peary as a hero, while the president of the Royal Geographic Society in London, England, stated that the commander's achievement was second "only to the attainment of the Pole."

Henson received very little mention in news stories, and he was usually described simply as "Peary's colored servant." However, he had not expected to be noticed, and he shrugged off the label of servant. He knew how valuable he had been to the expedition, and he felt delighted to be part of an enterprise that had won so much public acclaim. In addition, he had proved that a black person was just as capable as a white person of living in the Arctic. In his personal journal, Peary called Henson "my faithful colored boy" and said that he was "a hard worker and apt at anything, being in turn cook, hunter, dog driver, housekeeper, and bodyguard." It would be some years before Peary would find a far more appropriate title for Henson: "the best man I had with me."

For a few months in late 1892, Henson received treatment for the eye injury that he had suffered in Greenland. Dr. Cook referred him to an eye spe-

*A mirror image of Greenland's rugged coastline is captured in this photograph.*

*While Henson was recovering from an eye injury he had suffered in the Arctic, he stayed in Brooklyn, New York, (shown here) at the home of the sister of Dr. Frederick Cook.*

cialist, who diagnosed Henson's condition as sun blindness. The intense radiation of the sun's rays reflected off snow and ice had caused blisters to form on his damaged cornea. The blisters on Henson's eye had broken open, causing him pain when he opened and closed the eye. Cook arranged for Henson to recuperate at his sister's home in Brooklyn, and by December he had recovered the use of his eye and rejoined Peary.

Peary was busy raising money for his next trip to Greenland, and he needed Henson's help on a lecture tour that he was planning. Peary had brought a dog team back with him from Greenland, and he wanted Henson to drive a sledge around towns where a lecture was to be given to stir up interest in the event. At each stop on the tour, the stage of the local lecture hall was made to resemble an Eskimo village. Peary would give a talk illustrated with slides. When the slide show was finished, Peary would introduce his assistant, Matthew Henson. At that point, Henson would drive the dogs onto the stage. It was always the high point of the show, with members of the audience crowding close to touch the dogs.

One evening after a lecture in Philadelphia, Henson spotted the naval officer who had bet him that he would not return from the Arctic with all of his fingers and toes. After greeting the man, Henson showed him that all his digits were intact. Embarrassed about his previous remarks, the officer wrote Henson a check for $100.

*On his expeditions to the North, Peary often stopped at Eskimo settlements in Greenland to pick up supplies. Shown here, Eskimos hoist a dog team on board a ship.*

During a three-month period in late 1892, Peary and Henson made 165 lecture appearances and raised more than $20,000. After Peary had paid his debt from the previous expedition, he had $13,000 left for the next trip. General Isaac Wistar, the president of the Academy of Natural Sciences in Philadelphia, helped Peary obtain the leave he needed from the navy.

On June 26, 1893, a new expedition sailed from Philadelphia aboard the *Falcon*. Henson, Astrup, and Josephine Peary again accompanied Peary, but this time there were also 11 other members. Among the new recruits joining Peary were an artist to make paintings of Eskimo life, a taxidermist to stuff animal specimens for museum collections, and a nurse to care for the six-months-pregnant Josephine Peary. The *Falcon* put down anchor in an inlet just to the south of McCormick Bay, which the commander named Bowdoin Bay after the college in Maine that he had attended. On the site where Peary and his wife had

*Peary chose to establish his base for the 1893 expedition in Bowdoin Bay (shown here).*

spent their wedding anniversary the year before, Henson and other team members built a house. The building, which was much larger than Red Cliff House, was named Anniversary Lodge.

As usual, Henson had plenty of work to do. His first task was to build 10 sledges. Peary wanted them built very quickly because he was planning to deposit a large cache of supplies far out onto the ice cap before winter set in. He believed that the next spring's march would have a good chance of achieving its objective of exploring the northern coast of Greenland as long as the supplies were in place ahead of time.

Henson soon realized that the commander was regretting that he had brought 14 people with him on the expedition. Taking care of the needs of so many people was taxing to Peary. In addition, Josephine Peary would soon be giving birth to their first

*Inspecting the glacier near Bowdoin Bay in the summer of 1893, members of the Peary team search for a sledge route onto the ice cap.*

*Blizzards and bitterly cold temperatures took a heavy toll on the expedition members as they tried to pick their way around crevasses in the glaciers.*

child. Peary later admitted that he had been carried away by his enthusiasm while organizing the expedition, and he vowed that in the future he would bring smaller groups to the Arctic.

Fortunately for the overworked Henson, his Eskimo friends Ikwah, Ahnalka, and others of their tribe settled nearby on the bay. The good relations that he had established with the Eskimos were again useful. When his friends learned that he was too busy to hunt with them, they sat down and helped him to finish building the sledges.

When the sledges were ready, Peary sent Eivand Astrup and two other men, George Clark and Hugh Lee, up the glacier at the head of Bowdoin Bay. Their sledges were heavily loaded with food and provisions, and they were ordered to travel as far inland as possible before caching the supplies. A party of Eskimos went along with them as guides. The *Falcon* sailed home on August 20. Again, no supplies could come to the expedition from the outside until the following summer.

On September 12, Marie Ahnighito Peary was born. Eskimos traveled from as far away as 200 miles to see the white-skinned baby. However, little besides the birth of his daughter went right for Peary. Eskimos from the supply party hurried into camp with bad news. A storm had struck Astrup's advance group, which was trapped halfway up the glacier. Henson and Peary rushed to their relief and finally located the men in the midst of the still-raging storm. High winds had overturned two of the heavily laden sledges and blown them down the icy slopes. Peary and Henson found Clark and Astrup huddled behind the one remaining sledge. Clark's back was badly sprained, and Astrup was suffering from exposure and exhaustion. Hugh Lee had become separated from his companions, and his whereabouts were unknown. After three days of hard struggle, Henson and Peary managed to get the injured men back to Anniversary Lodge.

In the meantime, another disaster struck the expedition. The edge of the glacier hanging over the cliffs of Bowdoin Bay broke off and fell into the sea, sending a huge wave surging on shore and swamping the camp. Two boats were destroyed, and many fuel drums were washed away. The camp was soon put back in order, but another storm on the glacier prevented Henson from leading a search for Lee. As they were finally setting out, they met a group of Eskimos with Lee on a small sledge. He had wandered into their settlement after surviving for a week without food in the storms. He required six months of rest to recover from the frostbite he had suffered.

The long, dark winter settled in, and the morale among the expedition members was low. Because few forward caches had been laid down, Peary was doubtful that he would have enough time to carry out his plans for the next year. Henson went hunting with his Eskimo friends whenever the moonlight permit-

*Henson's strength and courage on the aborted trek to northern Greenland in 1894 helped to prevent a major disaster from occurring.*

ted, but the rest of the time he, too, could only wait for spring and hope that it would bring them better luck.

On March 6, 1894, the expedition got under way. This time Henson was in the party that ventured beyond the farthest advance caches, but he soon had to turn back to guide Lee and Astrup back to camp. The two men had again fallen victim to the extreme cold on the ice cap. Those who stayed with Peary did not fare much better. They encountered high winds and bitter temperatures as low as −50°F. As one of these hellish storms ended, another took its place. The men were unused to working in such cold, and they developed cases of frostbite and exhaustion. Many of the dogs died from *piblokto*, a disease also known as arctic distemper that affected humans as well as dogs.

Finally, on April 10, Peary gave the order to retreat. His group had traveled only 125 miles, about one-quarter of the way to its destination. Along the route back, the commander set up three caches containing tons of supplies and marked them with flags attached to 10-foot-long poles. Peary hoped to return later and make use of the provisions.

On April 21, the bedraggled, exhausted, and half-frozen men stumbled into camp. Henson helped the surgeon undress them and treat their frost injuries. The men had not been able to remove their clothes since the beginning of the expedition, and their bodies were covered with lice.

During the next few weeks, Henson watched as Peary sank into a depression. The commander had displayed courage and resolve too often in the past for Henson to believe that he would quit in the face of the present difficulties. Food caches were waiting out on the ice cap, and Henson was hopeful that the next expedition would have a better chance of success. He was determined that on the next trip he would accompany Peary all the way to the end.

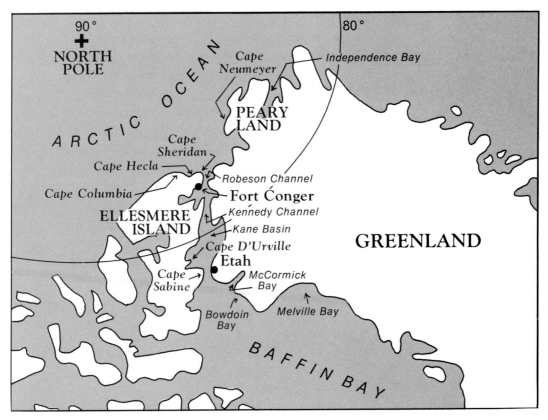

Henson had an idea that helped lift Peary's spirits. In 1818, the British explorer Captain James Ross had visited Melville Bay, more than 100 miles to the south. The Eskimos there had told Ross about large iron stones, or meteorites, that lay a little ways inland. However, no explorer had ever found the meteorites. Henson believed that if Peary could find them, he would be able to show some results that would satisfy his financial backers at home.

Henson found an Eskimo who could guide them to the meteorites, and he and Peary accompanied the Eskimo on a sledge ride down the coast to the site. The stones were far too large to move without cranes and pulleys. Peary decided to return for them another time. In the meantime. he chipped off enough pieces from them to whet the appetite of the American scientific community.

*This map illustrates features of the areas in northern Greenland visited by the Peary arctic expeditions.*

*Eskimo hunters skin a polar bear. Many of these native Greenland-ers settled near Peary's camp and traded their furs, fresh meat, and dog teams for knives, guns, and sewing needles.*

On August 3, a few days after Henson and Peary returned from their trek for the meteorites, the *Falcon* arrived at Bowdoin Bay. The ship did not bring any extra provisions because Peary had not expected to stay in Greenland. However, he nonetheless decided to remain there through the winter and make another try at a surveying trip during the next spring. Only Henson and Lee of all the team members volunteered to stay with the commander. The Arctic had broken the others.

By the end of the month, the ship was gone. With it went Josephine and Marie Peary. Money had to be raised to charter a ship for the next summer, and Peary's wife was planning to seek the funds from sci-entific organizations in the United States.

During the fall, the men made a trip onto the ice cap to check the nearest cache. Peary was horrified to find that severe weather had buried the supplies beyond any hope of recovery. The marker poles stood only six inches above the frozen surface. It seemed that Kokoyah was enjoying frustrating them.

To be able to march to Greenland's north coast in the spring, the men had to hunt extensively that fall. With the help of the Eskimos, they were suc-cessful in killing many walruses. They then mixed raisins and other dried fruit with the strips of walrus meat and dried all of it in the sun to make *pemmican*. This food was only a quarter as nutritious as beef, which meant that when traveling, they had to bring much more food for themselves and the dogs.

On April 1, 1895, Peary, Henson, and Lee left Anniversary Lodge for the ice cap. Henson was able to convince the Eskimos to help them carry supplies onto the ice cap as far as the largest cache. Ahnalka and his friends wanted as little as possible to do with Kokoyah's land. They felt certain it was only a matter of time before he would eat another interloper, just as he had disposed of John Verhoeff. On April 8,

when Ahnalka and his band turned back, he tried to convince Henson to come with them. He said it was foolish to go to a place where no animals lived or plants grew or fish swam. In the other direction were friends, women, warm dwellings, and plenty of food. Henson told his friend that he had to see for himself what lay ahead. He promised to come back and tell them what he had seen. They parted warmly, but Ahnalka was afraid that he was seeing Henson for the last time.

*During the fall of 1894, Henson and his Eskimo friends hunted walruses to provide meat for the next expedition. Shown here, Eskimo hunters drag a sledge loaded with musk-ox hides.*

The three men forged onward. They never found the caches that had been buried the previous year. This meant that all of the supplies they had were on their sledges. It would not take much more misfortune to make Ahnalka's prophecy come true, and at times it did seem that an angry devil was dogging their heels. The traveling proved difficult. They were battered by heavy winds, and the temperature often sank between $-30°F$ and $-50°F$.

The group moved with Peary driving a small sledge in the lead, navigating with his compass. Henson followed the commander with a huge sledge pulled

*In April 1895, Peary, Henson, and Hugh Lee set out for the north coast of Greenland with three sledges and dog teams. Henson skillfully handled most of the heavy driving.*

by 16 dogs, and Lee brought up the rear. Henson drove his sledge so well that in spite of his heavier load, he kept running up close behind Peary. He therefore suggested that his sledge be combined with the commander's to make a trailer sledge pulled by 28 dogs. He somehow managed to drive this tremendous load, which freed Peary to ski ahead and advance the trail faster.

Although brave and always willing to try his best, Lee lacked the strength and stamina of his companions. During a powerful storm, he became separated from them. Two days passed during which no travel was possible. Henson and Peary tried to keep warm in their tent. Twice a day they lit a stove, made tea, ate some pemmican, and fed the dogs.

The storm finally let up on the third day, and Henson went in search of Lee. He found the missing man a ways back on the trail, huddled on the equipment on top of his sledge. Lee had been nearly blinded by the windblown snow, and he was suffering from frostbite. Henson drove Lee and his team back to camp, all the time hearing Kokoyah's icy laughter in the wind, daring the men to continue.

After tending to Lee's injuries as best they could, they continued their trek. Lee's feet were so badly frostbitten that he could not stand. His sledge had to be abandoned, and he rode as a passenger on Henson's sledge. Many traveling days had been lost, and food was running dangerously low. After a while, there was not enough pemmican left to feed to the dogs. Following each day's march, Henson had to pick out the weakest dogs from the team, kill them with a blow from his hatchet, and feed the carcasses to the other dogs. He knew that when their food ran out, all three men would have to eat dog meat, too.

On the 36th day of the journey, they reached Navy Cliff, the part of the coast that Peary had explored three years before. Only one sledge and 11 scrawny dogs had survived the 600-mile ordeal. Henson knew that there was now no chance of exploring along the coast. The party would be in extreme peril unless the men had some success hunting and were met with better weather during their return to Bowdoin Bay.

Setting up Lee in the tent with most of the remaining food, Henson and Peary hiked down to the shore. The commander had sighted musk oxen in the area in 1892, and he was hoping that they were still around. Henson killed an arctic hare, and the famished men devoured it raw. A while later, they discovered a small herd of musk oxen. They crept up on the unsuspecting beasts and killed enough of them to provide hundreds of pounds of meat. However, when Peary started to skin a young animal he had shot, its mother attacked him. The commander ran for his life, calling to Henson to shoot the charging musk ox. Henson had just one chance to save Peary's life, for he had only one bullet left. He fired, dropping the animal a few yards from the commander. The relieved Peary praised his marksmanship. Henson, in turn, told the commander, "You sure can run."

After a few days of resting and eating to regain their strength, the party began the return journey back over the trail they had made on the way up. The meat they carried lasted until they were 200 miles from Bowdoin Bay. Henson killed and butchered all but one of the remaining dogs. As he undertook this gruesome job, he reflected that life in the Arctic was

an unbroken chain of violence, cold, and starvation. The strong lived by killing the weak. He spared the last dog to haul a sledge with the carcasses of its slaughtered teammates.

*Reaching Independence Bay on the north coast of Greenland in May 1895, the explorers gazed out at icebergs floating in the Arctic Sea.*

When they were 120 miles from Anniversary Lodge, Lee collapsed on the trail. Walking on snowshoes, he had been making a brave effort to keep up with them. Peary and Henson knew that one weak dog could not pull Lee back to camp on the sledge, so they picked up the traces on either side of the animal and began pulling Lee on the sledge on the final leg of their journey.

Finally, after 86 days on the ice cap, the near-dead men dragged themselves into Anniversary Lodge. They had eaten the last of the pemmican on the trek

*Nearly dead from hunger, exposure, and exhaustion, Peary's team finally returned to Anniversary Lodge on June 25, 1895.*

back, and they quickly consumed the small supply of food in the lodge. No one was well enough to hunt, and they all were suffering from malnutrition and exhaustion. Lee was in danger of dying from dysentery, a severe form of diarrhea. On the fifth day after their return, Nooktah, one of the local Eskimos, stopped by the lodge and found them. After Henson was given a bowl of broth, he bravely strapped himself onto Nooktah's sledge and drove several miles to the nearby Eskimo settlement to get help. Meanwhile, Nooktah took care of Peary and Lee.

As soon as Henson arrived at the settlement, he sent out a relief party to Anniversary Lodge. He stayed with the Eskimos for 10 days, receiving treatment and care from Kongolukso, the *angeeco*, or tribal medicine man. Kongolukso's wife fed him bowls of a broth made from seal's blood, which helped to relieve the effects of scurvy. This disease, which is caused by a deficiency of vitamin C in the diet, had weakened Henson's gums, making it difficult for him to chew. In about a week, he had regained his strength, and giving thanks to his benefactors, he returned to Bowdoin Bay.

Nooktah's initial amazement about the speed of Henson's recovery was dispelled when Henson told him that he had followed the *angeeco's* treatment. Under Nooktah's care, Peary had gotten much better, but Lee was still very ill. Despite his improving health, Peary's spirit had again sunk low. In fact, the ambitious lieutenant's mental state had sunk lower than ever, for he believed that he had nothing to show for his last two years in the North. He was doubtful that he would be able to win enough funding for a new expedition. Desperate to relieve Peary's gloom, Henson reminded him about the meteorites. If they were brought back to the United States, they might well generate interest in arctic exploration.

On August 3, the *Kite* arrived to bring the three men home. The *Falcon* had been lost at sea a few months before, and through lectures and constant appeals for money, Josephine Peary had managed to raise enough money to hire the ship used on the first expedition. On board the *Kite* was a doctor who was able to tend to Lee. Peary packed up souvenirs from his latest expedition and made plans for getting the meteorites.

The *Kite* sailed south to Melville Bay. A party of Eskimos came along to help in transporting the meteorites to the ship. The largest of the stones could not be moved, but the two smaller ones were dragged over the ground and the ice and hoisted aboard the *Kite*. After the Eskimos were paid for their work and taken back to their settlement, the ship sailed home.

The meteorites and the fine collection of skins that the expedition members had gathered were convincing evidence of the variety of natural treasures waiting to be wrested from the Arctic by whoever had the daring spirit to risk the adventure. Henson and Peary had that spirit in surplus. Before the *Kite* docked in New York, the commander told Henson that he planned to stay in the North for many years on the next expedition. He wanted to build a base as far north as possible so that he could make an attempt to reach the North Pole.

After returning to the United States, Peary and Henson learned that Fridtjof Nansen, a Norwegian explorer, had sailed to within 226 miles of the North Pole, 86° 14' north latitude. Nansen's ship, the *Fram*, had been specially constructed to ride on the ice of the Arctic Sea. On his expedition, Nansen had virtually proved that Greenland's land mass did not extend all the way to the Pole.

*While Peary and Lee lay in bed recovering from their 86-day ordeal on the ice cap, Henson drove a sledge to the nearby Eskimo settlement to get help.*

Peary, who did not want Nansen or anyone else to beat him to the North Pole, knew that he could count on Henson when needed. During the last expedition, he had discovered that Henson was the one man whose services were indispensable in helping him get to the Pole. Only Henson had proved himself to have the strength and the endurance to survive on the march to the top of the world.

Both men were united in their commitment to the quest. Together they had faced the devils of the North, and the Arctic was still in their blood. ✤

*Peary's expedition returned to the United States with two meteorites as souvenirs of the Arctic; but the largest meteorite (shown here) had to be left behind.*

# 5

# A SERIES
# OF SETBACKS

JUST AS HENSON had predicted, Peary received plenty of acclaim when he returned to the United States with the meteorites in September 1895. Funds for future trips were assured, although getting another leave of absence from the navy was difficult for Peary. However, his friends were finally able to convince the secretary of the navy to give him more time off.

As plans were being made for the next expedition, Henson took a job at the American Museum of Natural History in New York City. A member of the museum's staff had seen the collection of stuffed and mounted animals that Peary had brought back from the Arctic and was impressed by the work that Henson had done skinning the animals. The man asked Henson to assist him in setting up an exhibition of the collection in the museum. His job at the museum was a sharp contrast to his work in the Arctic. But while he was in New York, he made many friends in the black community. Among them was George Gardner, the chief shipping clerk for a large textile firm, who helped Henson understand how important his work with Peary was to the pride of black Americans.

While working at the museum, Henson waited for Peary to call him to action, and the call soon came. Peary decided that before he made an attempt to reach the North Pole, he would retrieve the large

*Icicles hang from the walls of a cavern inside an iceberg off the coast of Antarctica. This photograph was taken during the British explorer Robert Scott's tragic 1911–12 expedition to the South Pole.*

*While waiting for Peary's next expedition to begin, Henson took a job with the American Museum of Natural History in New York and helped to set up an exhibit devoted to life in the Arctic.*

meteorite that had to be left in Greenland in 1895. During both 1896 and 1897, Henson sailed with Peary to Melville Bay on board the ship *Hope*. On the first trip, the ice pack covering the sea was too thick, and the ship had to turn back. They secured the 35-ton trophy on the second expedition and brought it back to the Museum of Natural History, where it is still on display.

Riding the crest of his fame, Peary made a public statement on January 12, 1897, that he intended to reach the North Pole. His friend Morris Jesup, the president of the American Geographical Society and the Museum of Natural History, organized a group of businessmen to form the Peary Arctic Club, which would provide financial support for the explorer. Peary

explained that his plan was to sail in a ship strong enough to batter its way through ice floes clear up through Kennedy and Robeson channels, the northernmost portions of the waterways that lay between Greenland and Ellesmere Island. From this region on the northwest coast of Greenland, Peary intended to create bases from which an expedition to the Pole could be launched. He realized that he had taken too many people with him on the 1893 expedition, and on his next attempt his team would include only two other men, Henson and a surgeon, Thomas Dedrick.

Unexpectedly, Henson now felt hesitant about spending four more years in the North. He was enjoying his life in New York, and he had begun to save money. He even had some thoughts about get-

*Much like the man shown here shooting at a walrus from the deck of a ship, Henson was kept busy hunting game while he was in the North.*

ting married. When George Gardner heard that he was unsure whether or not to join the expedition, his friend impressed on him how important it was for blacks to have national heroes like the man who would accompany Peary to the North Pole. This chance to elevate the racial pride of his people helped Henson to cast aside doubts he had about again submitting himself to the hardships of the Arctic.

Early in the summer of 1898, the expedition got under way on board the *Hope*. Gardner was at the docks to see Henson off and gave him a pair of thick woolen mittens that would give him a good grip, Gardner said, for when he was "climbing up the North Pole."

The expedition included two ships. In addition to the *Hope*, which returned home after leaving the team in Greenland, Peary had the *Windward*, a ship that had been donated to the expedition by a wealthy British publisher. Peary hoped that this ship would be strong enough to take him north of Ellesmere Island, but its engines soon proved to be too weak for the task. After picking up Eskimo helpers and dog teams, the expedition stopped at Etah, one of the most northerly of the Eskimo settlements. From there, the *Windward* tried to force a passage northward. Peary's luck was again very bad. Ice in the channels grew so thick that the ship became frozen fast off Cape D'Urville of Ellesmere Island, about 400 miles south of the point that Peary had hoped to reach.

A change of plans was necessary. Peary decided that they would march north to Fort Conger, an abandoned building on the northern part of Ellesmere Island. There they would make their advance base. Fort Conger was the place where the members of the ill-fated Greely expedition had waited in vain to be rescued in 1883. They had finally been forced to march south from the fort, and most of the men had died before being rescued.

In the fall of 1898, Peary made preparations for the march to Fort Conger. He spent most of his time supervising hunting parties and checking the work of the Eskimo women who were making the men's extra-warm fur outfits. Henson had the important job of starting a trail to Fort Conger. Working in temperatures colder than −60°F, he and his Eskimo assistants cut a trail and set up camps with igloos and stocks of food and fuel. Much of the route had to pass over the sea ice in Kane Basin, the waterway on which Cape D'Urville was located, and the work was backbreaking because the ice rarely stayed smooth for any distance on the frozen bays and channels. All along the way, the men had to go over and around places where the ice jutted up in huge jagged lines, presenting an incredible obstacle course to travelers. These areas, known as pressure ridges, are created when strong arctic winds force ice floes to smash into one another.

*In 1896 and 1897, Henson sailed with Peary on the* Hope *(shown here) to retrieve the huge meteorite that was left behind in Greenland in 1895.*

*Henson had to wait for a month and a half—until the sun crept high enough over the horizon—before he could return south with the badly injured Peary.*

Fort Conger lay 250 miles north of Cape D'Urville. At first, Peary had planned to occupy it after the winter. But the appearance in the area of another explorer, the Norwegian Otto Sverdrup, changed Peary's mind. He decided that he must get to the fort immediately or Sverdrup would beat him to it. Henson advised Peary that they should wait at least until February, when the sun rose a little higher above the horizon. However, Peary refused to wait.

Leaving Dr. Dedrick aboard the icebound *Windward*, Henson, Peary, and four Eskimos started out for Fort Conger in December 1898. The trail that Henson had made during the previous months ended halfway to the fort, and from there the traveling was extremely difficult. The temperature stayed below −60°F as they hacked their way north in the dark, judging their position by the number of inlets and bays they had crossed. To make matters worse, they ran out of food 50 miles from the fort, and Henson had to kill a dog for them to eat. The men finally reached the dilapidated and drift-covered building known as Fort Conger just after midnight on January 6, 1899.

Once inside, sheltered from the weather, the men made a meal of supplies that had stayed preserved there since 1893: salt pork and the almost unpalatable biscuit known as hardtack. Henson built a fire that brought the temperature in the building up to a comfortable level. It was then that Peary complained he had a wooden feeling in his feet. Henson helped him remove his boots and the inner boot liners. However, part of the boot liners remained stuck to Peary's feet. As Henson cut away the liners where they were stuck to Peary's feet, he was appalled to see that the tips of several of the commander's frostbitten toes came off with the material.

In addition to being frostbitten, Peary's feet were also infected with gangrene poisoning. He would almost certainly have died from gangrene if Henson had not known how to care for the commander's frozen feet. Gradually warming Peary's toes until the blood again began to circulate through them, Henson administered antiseptic to the purplish flesh to keep the infection from spreading. During the next weeks, while Peary lay in bed in horrible agony, Henson waited for better weather and the return of the sun.

To add to his troubles, Henson had to quell a rebellion among the Eskimos, who wanted to leave Fort Conger immediately. Their dogs were dying on a diet of just salt pork, and Peary's disability had convinced them that the party was doomed. Henson knew that he had to have their help in getting Peary back to the ship, so he decided to make them an offer. He would lead a hunting expedition, and if they were successful in finding game, then the men would stay. The Eskimos scoffed at him, believing that no animals would be found at that time of year so far to the north. But Henson was able to organize a hunt, and they found a herd of musk oxen, which provided them with the food they needed. The Eskimos praised Henson's great skill at hunting and abandoned their talk about leaving.

By February 18, 1899, there was enough light to travel. Henson lashed Peary to a sledge, and in 11 days he drove the 250 miles back to the *Windward*. Four weeks later, Dr. Dedrick, with Henson assisting him, amputated all but the little toes on both of Peary's feet.

The *Windward* sailed for home early in August, dropping Peary and Henson off at the Etah Eskimo settlement, where they spent the winter. Peary was not about to be stopped by his latest setback, and he made plans for further expeditions from Fort Conger. Within weeks of the operation, he was moving around on crutches. Later, he had Henson lash him to a sledge so that he could come along on the trips to supply Fort Conger.

By March 1900, Peary, Henson, and six Eskimos were again based at Fort Conger. Peary planned to travel along the north coast of Greenland and find a point from which an expedition to the Pole could be mounted. Seven sledges left the fort on April 9. The team crossed from Ellesmere Island to Greenland over Kennedy Channel and then cut north onto the Arctic Sea ice, skirting the coast as they advanced. As sup-

plies were used up, the Eskimo helpers returned one by one to Fort Conger with nearly empty sledges. The party eventually consisted of Henson, Peary, and two Eskimos. A new spit of land was discovered, which Peary named Cape Morris K. Jesup, in honor of his friend and supporter.

At the farthest point north that they had reached until then, the men ventured far out onto the sea ice, moving slowly toward the North Pole. Their progress was soon impeded by jagged and broken ice floes. Food supplies dwindled, and the Eskimos became frightened of the sea-ice region. They said that it was the territory of another powerful devil, Tahnusuk. At 83° 59' north latitude off Greenland's north coast, the team turned back. Henson led the return journey. Sixty days after their departure from Fort Conger, they were back at the base. Peary needed help to stand and walk inside the building, and he thanked Henson for doing so much of the work on the trip.

Although the expedition had not come close to reaching the North Pole, Peary was satisfied because he had finally mapped the last unexplored areas on the north coast of Greenland. He now knew for cer-

*In the spring of 1900, Peary, Henson, and a team of Eskimos traveled along the north coast of Greenland during their unsuccessful attempt to reach the North Pole.*

tain that the only route to the Pole lay across the vast, treacherous expanse of the Arctic Sea. The next expedition would leave from bases that he planned to establish on northern Ellesmere Island.

In order to have enough time to reach the North Pole during the extremely short summer at the top of the world, Peary decided that the team must spend the winter at Fort Conger. Again, Henson led a team of Eskimos in successful hunts of musk oxen and caribou, and they soon had enough meat for the next expedition. They also discovered a seam of coal near the fort, which provided all the fuel they needed for their extended stay. Henson did the best job he could to recondition the sledges for their upcoming journey across the polar-sea ice. With no wood available with which to make repairs, he was not able to do as complete a job as he would have liked.

On April 5, 1901, Peary and Henson set off from Fort Conger on a journey that they hoped would end at the North Pole. Only one of the Eskimos, a man named Sipsoo, agreed to go with them on the trip across the polar-sea ice. The others feared Tahnusuk too much. They were convinced the three men were suffering from piblokto and were sure to die.

*Peary and Henson traveled along the last unexplored area of Greenland's north coast in 1900, proving that the land mass did not extend farther north toward the Pole.*

Henson, Peary, and Sipsoo traveled with two heavily loaded sledges. Henson went first, breaking a trail through the snow and ice. Peary followed him, weakly shuffling along on his injured feet. They only got as far as Cape Hecla, one of Ellesmere's northernmost points. Ahead lay the Arctic Sea, heaving under its icy coat. The North Pole beckoned more than 500 hundred miles farther on, but there was no chance of reaching it. Their sledges were too weak to stand up against the rugged sea-ice conditions. They had to turn back. The third attempt in their planned four-year siege of the Pole had lasted only eight days.

After the team returned to Fort Conger, Peary learned that the Peary Arctic Club had sent the *Windward* to check on his situation. The ship had spent the past winter anchored far to the south of Fort Conger. Among those on the ship was Josephine Peary. The explorers immediately left their northern base to meet the ship. As Henson witnessed the reunion between Peary and his wife, he felt twinges of his former reluctance to make the trip. He wondered when he would allow himself to enjoy the pleasures of family life. He comforted himself with the thought that at least he was living an adventurous life, one that might bring him worldwide fame and fortune. At home, he would have no such opportunity.

The *Windward* sailed for the United States in August 1901. Peary insisted on making one more attempt at the Pole. An enclosed structure on the *Windward* known as the deckhouse had been hoisted ashore on an area of central Ellesmere Island called Cape Sabine. There Peary planned to gather supplies for the next expedition.

During the winter, Henson again made many hunting trips. Early in 1902, he began to move supplies up to the fort. In late February, Peary and four Eskimos joined him at the fort, and preparations were

Henson stands beside a sledge on the deck of a ship. In the spring of 1901, he and Peary traveled from Fort Conger to meet the supply ship Windward *and its passengers, who included Josephine Peary.*

*Peary (shown here) was unable to persuade the team's Eskimo helpers to venture onto the polar-sea ice, but Henson convinced the men that the U.S. Navy ''devil'' was mightier than the sea-ice devil.*

begun for transporting supplies to the last land camp on Cape Hecla. The next few weeks were spent preparing the sledges for the trip.

On March 23, the eve of their departure, the Eskimos mutinied. They sat by their sledges and refused to load them. Peary could not induce them to work. Offers of extra presents of valuable goods were turned down. He was told that all of the fine gifts in the world were no good to people whom Tahnusuk was going to eat. Peary tried to reason with them, saying that it was obvious that no such devil existed because no one had ever seen him. The Eskimos responded by telling Peary that Tahnusuk had thwarted him again and again on the sea ice. The devil had robbed Peary of his toes, starved him, killed his dogs. How, they demanded, could he dare to say that Tahnusuk did not exist?

Peary was stymied. He sent Henson to talk to the Eskimos. A short time later, Henson returned and told Peary that everything was all right. The Eskimos were packing their sledges. When the commander asked how he had convinced them to change their minds, Henson smiled broadly and explained. He had told the Eskimos that in the south lived a devil even greater than Tahnusuk: the U.S. Navy. Peary, he said, was a favorite of this southern devil; therefore, Tahnusuk could never defeat him.

On April 6, 1902, the men left Cape Hecla and headed out onto the sea ice. Temperatures immediately plummeted. For days, the dog teams struggled to pull the sledges through deep snow and up and over huge pressure ridges. The Arctic Sea's ice coating was broken in some places, and ice floes floated in the gaps. On some days, Peary's team managed to move only three miles after 16 hours of backbreaking work. Once, in the middle of the night, the ice floe they were camped on split apart with a sharp crack like a rifle shot. Some of the Eskimos had been sleeping on the other part of the ice floe, and Henson and Peary shouted directions to them to paddle with their snowshoes until the ice floes moved back together.

Traveling on the ice was often a very frightening experience. A patch of open water, which on the sea ice was known as a lead, could appear suddenly, whereas moments before the ice had seemed solid. The leads were usually narrow, measuring five or six feet across. The dogs and the men could jump across them, and the 12-foot-long sledges could bridge them and be hauled across to safety. Sometimes, wider leads that had just refrozen would barely support their weight, and dogs and men would cross a surface that swayed and bounced under their feet. Henson thought that the ever-present danger of falling into a lead best explained the Eskimos' belief in the devil Tahnusuk.

In addition to the perils of the ice surface, the men also faced the problem of determining which way was north. Compasses are strongly affected by constantly changing magnetic variations near the poles, and needles will sometimes indicate that north lies in a direction that is really to the south, east, or west. Only by observing the position of the sun at noon with an instrument known as a sextant can explorers be certain in which direction north lies.

After two weeks of traveling, the team came to a lead as wide as a big river. It stretched east and west as far as they could see. The only thing they could do was to set up camp and wait for the water to refreeze. Peary decided to send two Eskimos back to Fort Conger in order to conserve the remaining food. As they waited, terrible storms lashed the camp. The dogs came down with piblokto and began to die at an alarming rate. Eventually, the men reached the point where they did not have enough food to get to the Pole and back. Their latitude was 84° 17'.

On April 21, barely a month after leaving Fort Conger, Peary wrote in his journal, "The game is off.

*In April 1902, Henson (shown here), Peary, and their Eskimo helpers set out from the north coast of Ellesmere Island in another attempt to reach the Pole.*

My dream of sixteen years is ended. . . . I have made the best fight I know. I believe it has been a good one. I cannot accomplish the impossible."

Henson took in the gloomy situation quietly. He, too, felt helpless and frustrated. There was nothing to say. He loaded his sledge, readied his dog team, and led the march back.

Once on land, Peary told Henson that he knew of a way to solve their problems. They needed a ship that could sail them and their supplies as far north as Cape Hecla. This would eliminate having to break hundreds of miles of trails just to haul supplies to the departure point. No such ship existed, but Peary vowed that he would design one and see that it was built.

After reaching the *Windward*, which had returned to bring the men home, Peary heard some upsetting news. An Italian expedition led by Luigi Amadeo

*Henson (shown here) led the march back to land after the team's failure to reach the North Pole in 1902.*

and Umberto Cagni claimed to have reached 86° 34',
which was closer to the Pole than Fridtjof Nansen's
previous record. It was also 120 miles farther than
Henson and Peary had gone. Their most recent trip
on the sea ice now seemed unimportant. But rather
than being crushed by the news of Amadeo and Cagni's achievement, Peary felt spurred onward by this
new challenge. Henson believed that only death could
make him and Peary give up their quest for the Pole,
even though the hard work and the arctic climate
were taking their toll.

As the two men began their voyage home, Henson looked at Peary, a tall and somber figure on the
deck, tottering a little on his crippled feet like a
stunned boxer who refuses to go down. Henson turned
away silently and went down to his cabin. This round
was over, but the fight would continue. **⟨⟩**

*As he sailed for home in 1902,
Peary was already making plans
for building a ship that would be
strong enough to carry an expedition to the Arctic Sea.*

# 6

## ALMOST
## THERE

❧

IN THE FALL of 1902, back in the United States once more, Henson decided to strike out on his own for a while. Peary would need years to gather the funds necessary for a new expedition and have his specially built ship constructed. There was little that Henson could do to help Peary, who had no money to spare for his assistant.

The 36-year-old Henson did not mind having time off from arctic exploration. He wanted to travel throughout the United States, and he took a job with the Pennsylvania Railroad, working as a porter on the Pullman sleeping cars. Making hundreds of runs, he traveled extensively on train routes from New England to the Midwest. Then, deciding to change routes so he could see another part of the country, he transferred to a West Coast train. But before he headed out west, he boarded a train that was making a run to Florida.

The South delighted Henson. Florida's abundant sunshine, colorful architecture, and endless orchards of fruit trees instantly appealed to him. When his train stopped for a day in Fort Meyers, Florida, he decided to visit an orchard and pick an orange.

He did not have to go far to get his fruit. An orange came flying from across the tracks, where some white workers were loading train cars with crates of

*After returning to the United States in 1902, Henson took a job as a pullman porter with the Pennsylvania Railroad.*

*Angered by the racial hostility he encountered while working on trains in the South, Henson returned to New York City. This photograph shows downtown Brooklyn at the turn of the century.*

fruit. The orange hit him in the back, and it was followed by a barrage of other pieces of fruit. Henson ran back to the train, with the workers yelling after him "that niggers weren't welcome in Fort Meyers."

After his anger cooled a little, Henson decided that it was best to forget about the incident. He sat down in a passenger seat and started reading an article in a magazine. The article was about Peary, whom the writer described as a "deluded fanatic" who was building a new ship to continue his hopeless chase of the North Pole. Engrossed in his reading, Henson did not raise his head until nightfall.

As Henson reached out to pull down his window shade, he heard voices on the darkened platform. Pressing his face to the glass, he saw three whites walking alongside the train, scanning the windows. One of them carried something that appeared to be a stick. When the men spotted Henson, one of them yelled, "Get the black bastard." Henson saw that the stick was a shotgun. He immediately threw himself to the floor, just in time to escape the gun blast that shattered the window, showering the car with broken glass. "That'll teach them we don't like niggers down here," one of the men declared.

After again being attacked by hostile whites during a stopover in New Orleans, Louisiana, Henson decided to quit his job and return to New York. There he waited for a call from Peary. After his trip through the South, Henson was feeling upset and disappointed about the lack of progress that had been made about the racial situation in America. It hurt him terribly that his skin color should make him the target of violence in his own country. The years in the Far North had accustomed him to accept people based on their abilities and characters, not their looks.

Before long, a letter came from Peary. His new ship would be arriving in New York in March 1905. He had named it the *Roosevelt* after President Theodore Roosevelt, who was one of Peary's strongest backers. Peary wrote that he hoped Henson would come aboard and help prepare the ship to sail in July.

*Work begins on the* Roosevelt, *the specially designed ship that Peary intended to sail into the polar sea region.*

*Eskimos gather beside an ice-bound ship. Much of the preparatory work for the 1906 expedition was performed by Henson and his teams of Eskimo assistants.*

In the meantime, Henson resumed his friendship with George Gardner. At a party at Gardner's home, he met Lucy Ross, an attractive, strong-minded young woman, who worked as a clerk at a bank. They began to see each other often, and Henson soon realized that he had fallen in love. He asked Lucy to marry him and was surprised when she consented. When he explained that he had little money, she said that she did not care. Overjoyed about his engagement, Henson went to meet the *Roosevelt* with a new feeling of confidence. He vowed to bring Lucy the North Pole as a wedding present.

On board the *Roosevelt*, Henson met the newcomers to Peary's team: Ross Marvin, a Cornell University professor; Louis Wolf, the ship's surgeon; and Robert Bartlett, an Englishman who was to be the captain of the ship. Peary told them that Henson would be their instructor about life in the Arctic.

Leaving New York on June 16, 1905, the ship stopped at Etah to pick up Eskimos and dogs. Then the *Roosevelt* did the work she had been created to do: challenge the ice-choked waters leading to northern Ellesmere Island. Two weeks of ice-crunching travel gained them an anchorage at Cape Sheridan, which was near the outlet to the Arctic Ocean. The first part of the mission was a success.

The fall and winter of 1905 were devoted to getting the men into condition for the trek and stockpiling game for the expedition in the spring. Henson oversaw the work of the Eskimos, who were preparing garments, sledges, and food supplies. Peary attended to the work of planning a strategy for their assault on the Pole.

Calling the men together, Peary explained his tactics. Two groups would be formed. An advance party would break a trail with lightly loaded sledges, moving steadily toward the Pole. The main party, which would be divided into smaller groups, would follow them with heavier-loaded sledges. Teams from the main party would continually return to land to pick up more supplies. Thus, a relay team would be established to ferry supplies over a well-worn trail ever farther out onto the Arctic Ocean's ice cap. To Henson, Peary's plan seemed to be a foolproof strategy for avoiding the supply problems that had hindered them in the past.

On March 1, 1906, Henson and two Eskimos, Seegloo and Ootah, ventured onto the sea ice and started the trail. Peary planned to leave with the main party six days later. Soon after his departure, it became clear to Henson that the expedition was in trouble. Fierce winds blew at them from the northwest, and the sea ice began to drift toward the southeast. The trail that Henson's party left began to break apart as ice floes separated. Unusually warm temperatures caused many troublesome leads to open in the

The Roosevelt *lies anchored in ice off the coast of Cape Sheridan, the point from which Peary launched his march onto the polar sea in the spring of 1906.*

*Strong winds and unusually warm temperatures caused large open areas of water, known as leads, to form along the route Peary's team took across the polar-sea ice.*

ice. One day, Henson's party had to cross 14 leads in a 10-mile stretch.

On March 26, Henson's team was stopped by a lead that was a half-mile wide. When Peary caught up to them and took a latitude reading, he became convinced it was the same open water that had stopped them in 1902. They made camp on the lead's southern edge, waiting for more groups from the main party to reach them. After a four-day delay, they were able to cross the gap. Then a blizzard held them up for six days, forcing them to construct igloos for shelter.

Peary checked their position after the storm. They had drifted steadily eastward for more than 70 miles. Instead of being north of Ellesmere Island, they were above Greenland. The rest of the teams would probably never find them. Their supply line was cut, and the foolproof plan was blown apart by the unpredictable arctic weather.

For a brief time, Henson and Peary pushed onward. While many of their dogs died, the men refused
to stop, continuing on with too little food and too
little sleep. On April 21, 52 days after Henson had
started out, Peary called him to halt. His observations
showed them to be at 87° 6' north latitude. It was a
new record. They were 175 miles from the Pole.
However, they had to turn back: With any luck, they
might have just enough food to reach the ship.

As Henson had done so often in the past, he took
charge of the return to land. He inspired the frightened Eskimos to keep working and pushed men and
dogs to the limits of their endurance. They again
encountered the gaping lead they had crossed on the
way north. They waited there for five excruciating
days while their food supplies dwindled. Finally, a
thin coat of ice formed over the lead. Men and dogs
inched across, sliding rather than lifting their feet.

In a letter written in August 1906, Peary recorded events from the Roosevelt's harrowing return journey southward.

The newly formed ice rippled beneath them. At the lead's southern edge, they looked back and saw their sledge tracks filling up with water. They had made it across just in time.

The men finally reached land at Cape Neumeyer in northern Greenland. Peary immediately led a hunt that netted them plenty of fresh game. The famished men and dogs ate the meat and then turned their weary steps west toward Cape Sheridan. On their way back along the coast, they found all of the men from the other groups. Eighty-one days after leaving land, Henson and the rest of his team were again aboard the Roosevelt. During the arduous trek, Henson's weight had gone from his usual 150 pounds to 100 pounds.

*A moonlit photograph of the Roosevelt. When Henson returned to the United States in 1906, he knew that the next attempt to reach the Pole would be his and Peary's last.*

Even after returning to the ship, the men were not out of danger. The *Roosevelt* had been severely damaged by the crushing weight of an ice pack that it was moored on. During the summer, the ship managed to break free from the melting ice and work its way south with difficulty. The expedition finally reached New York on December 24, 1906.

To the surprise of nearly everybody except Henson, Peary confidently announced that he was just back for repairs. He planned soon to resume his quest to claim the Pole for the United States. However, the commander confided to Henson that the next attempt would be their last. The years of hardship had taken too much out of him to make more than one additional voyage north. Peary was 50 years old, and he felt battered and exhausted in body and mind.

In September 1907, Henson married Lucy Ross. However, their time together was short. He was soon back on the *Roosevelt*, helping to oversee the completion of repairs on the ship. Peary and Henson would be sailing north for the last time in July 1908. ☙

# 7

# AT LAST!

——— ✦ ———

THE NEW MEMBERS of Peary's team were George Borup, Dr. J. W. Goodsell, and Donald MacMillan. Returning from the 1906 expedition were Ross Marvin and Captain Bob Bartlett, both of whom had become veterans of Arctic Sea ice travel during the previous trek. All of the men were young, and they were extremely confident that the expedition would be a success. Henson looked upon the younger men with a practiced eye, trying to judge their capabilities. He was 42 years old, and he had no illusions about life in the Arctic or the dangers that the team would be facing. He had seen too many disfiguring injuries and had been near death too many times to face the new venture with anything except extreme caution.

The expedition left New York on July 6, 1908, stopping first at Oyster Bay, New York. President Theodore Roosevelt, who was on vacation at his nearby family estate, came aboard the ship that bore his name and gave his good wishes to each member of the team. The president told Peary, "If any man succeeds in reaching the Pole, you'll be that man."

Henson prayed that he would be with Peary all the way to the end of the journey. He knew that this would be his last adventure, his last chance to win glory for himself and all black Americans.

---

*Henson made his last trip to Greenland—where he saw sunsets like the one shown here—in 1908, when he was 42 years old.*

*Bidding good luck to the crew of the ship that bore his name, President Theodore Roosevelt (center, in white suit) looks into the compartment where dogs were kept on the journey north.*

Again, the usual preparations were made on the voyage north. Eskimo helpers and dog teams were taken aboard in Greenland, and equipment was readied for the expedition. On September 5, 1908, the *Roosevelt* was anchored off Cape Sheridan.

As Henson looked out over the Arctic Sea ice, he reflected that even with all his years of experience in arctic exploration, he had no way of knowing whether the trip back from Cape Sheridan would be made in joy or sorrow. In choosing a life of adventure, he knew that few things could ever be certain for him. His work duties soon removed any time he had for further reflection. He gave the newcomers to the team thorough instruction in how to live and work in the Arctic. As part of the training, the men transported supplies farther west down the coast to Cape Columbia, establishing a camp there called Crane City.

On February 27, Peary gathered the men at Crane City and gave them a pep talk. His words, while not rousing, did inspire them with confidence. Later, the men met in Bartlett's igloo. They toasted each other with brandy and sang their college songs. Henson slipped out into the night. These songs had no meaning to him. His college had been the Arctic. The time had come to prove how well he had mastered its lessons.

The next day, Bartlett and Borup started out with the advance party that would break the trail for the other groups. Henson and his Eskimo helpers followed one day later. For a quarter of a mile, they followed the advance party's path over the jagged ice near the shore. Almost immediately, they had to pull out axes and chop their way through particularly rough areas. Henson's sledge split after only a mile, and he was forced to make emergency repairs in the face of a tremendous wind.

At the end of the first day of travel, they took shelter in an igloo that Bartlett and Borup had made at the end of their first march. The igloo was only 12 miles from shore. They still had more than 400 miles to go. In a diary account he was keeping, Henson wrote about how ferocious the wind had been on the first day. "No other but a Peary party would have attempted to travel in such weather," he noted. He also wrote that temperatures on the sea ice were especially frigid: "All through the night I would wake from the cold and beat my arms or feet to keep the circulation going."

In a few days, the traveling improved greatly, and Henson noted that he had never seen smoother sea ice. They finally caught up to the advance party, which had been stopped by a wide lead. With the exception of the rear party led by Marvin and Borup, the other groups soon reached the lead, and a camp of igloos began to grow.

*Bartlett's advance team builds an igloo on the polar ice. Members of the expedition traveled in separate teams on their way to the Pole.*

Bob Bartlett (shown here) was the last member of the expedition whom Peary sent back to land. Henson and four Eskimos were asked to accompany the commander to the Pole.

On March 5, the sun became visible for the first time that year—a crimson sphere skimming just above the southern horizon. The weather became frustratingly warm, with temperatures reaching almost 0°F. Before them, the open water spread a mile or more into the distance. Henson sat there impatiently, knowing that they needed to travel 20–25 miles a day to keep on schedule. He wrote: "We eat and sleep, and watch the lead and wonder. . . . Are we to be repulsed again?"

Bartlett fumed during the delay, calling their camp "hell on earth." Only MacMillan remained cheerful, and he tried to keep the other men amused with his endless supply of stories and jokes. With Henson's help, MacMillan organized games and competitions among the Eskimos to keep them interested in the expedition. The prizes that MacMillan offered to winners of various events were parts of the *Roosevelt*: the rudder, spars, anchors, and keel. No one cared that the prizes were all nonsense; the games had cut through the tension.

Finally, on March 11, the temperature plunged to nearly −50°F, and ice formed on the lead. Bartlett's group crossed first, and the other groups followed a few hours later. The Marvin and Borup party, which was bringing the last of the supplies, still had not appeared. Peary left a note in one of the igloos telling them to hurry.

The ice remained fairly smooth, and the groups traveled fast. On the morning of March 14, Marvin and Borup overtook Henson and Peary's groups, bringing them badly needed supplies. Shortly after the rear party arrived, Peary sent Goodsell and some Eskimos back to the *Roosevelt* with a sledge that carried just enough supplies to get the team back to shore. The commander had begun the process of thinning down the expedition. After every march of five days, he planned to send one of the team members back to land with a group of Eskimos. He was cal-

*Delayed for a week in early March 1909 by a wide lead, the men released their tension by participating in contests organized by Donald MacMillan and Henson.*

culating on preserving just enough supplies to allow a few men to reach the Pole. However, no one—not even Henson—knew who Peary would choose to stay with him until the end.

As the march continued, the weather remained extremely cold. For 12 hours a day, Henson and the others lifted and dragged their sledges through hip-deep snow, over small leads, and across jagged ice floes. Two sledges split in half, forcing the men to stop and make time-consuming repairs. In the bitter cold, Henson worked without gloves on his hands, drilling holes to fit leather thongs through the sledges.

MacMillan, whose heel became badly frozen, went south on March 15. Borup's turn came five days later. The tension between the remaining explorers mounted, although they all were too dedicated to the success of the team to demand to know who would be asked to go to the Pole. Bartlett and Henson continued ahead as the trailblazers. In addition to his work advancing the trail, Bartlett was making measurements with a sextant to determine their latitude. After Bartlett and Henson advanced the trail a day's march ahead, they would build an igloo, eat, and go to sleep.

*Unable to walk for long distances because of his crippled feet, Peary was forced to ride in a sledge during much of the 1909 expedition.*

While they slept, Peary, Marvin, and the Eskimos marched on the trail that the advance group had created. Thus, at least one party was traveling at all times.

On March 25, Peary gave Marvin and two Eskimos orders to return to land. Henson breathed a sigh of relief. He knew that one more party would be sent back and either he or Bartlett would be put in charge of it. He hoped that Peary would choose Bartlett.

Peary, Henson, and Bartlett each took command of one of the sledges as they continued their advance on the Pole. All three parties had healthy dogs and plenty of food and fuel. For days they sped along, averaging 16 miles a march. On March 28, they passed beyond the farthest point that they had reached on the 1906 trek. Now every mile covered set a new record.

Five more days of travel passed, and on March 30, Peary told Bartlett to return south. Peary, Henson, and four Eskimos—Seegloo, Ootah, Egingwah, and Ooqueah—would make the final dash to the Pole. Bartlett was disappointed, but he congratulated Henson.

"There's no man in the world right this minute with a greater responsibility than you, Henson," Bartlett said. "The commander is tired. We've done all we can. The rest is up to you. History will be made in these next few days."

Henson well understood Bartlett's frustration about coming so close to the Pole only to have to turn back.

He said, "Don't worry, Captain. We'll make it."

They shook hands, and Bartlett left with his group on the long journey back. Soon all they could see of his team was the steamy breath of his dogs hanging in the air to the south.

On April 1, the six men who would make the final march started their trek. For Peary and Henson, the ultimate prize and the reason for all their efforts and sacrifices during the last 18 years lay only 130 miles away. Peary had to travel much of the way riding on a sledge because he was unable to march for long on his crippled feet. But his determination to achieve his goal propelled him onward. Henson set a ferocious pace on the last five-day march. In order to cover the distance to the Pole, they needed to average an incredible 26 miles a day.

The temperature rose to almost −15°F. Henson was worried that the team would encounter an un-crossable lead, and he pushed his companions to work 20 hours a day. At the end of April 5, Henson es-timated that they had only 35 miles to go.

That night, only the Eskimos could sleep deeply. Henson and Peary tossed restlessly all night. After a few hours, Peary woke up Henson. It was time to go. Henson rose immediately, roused Seegloo and Ootah, and began breaking the final trail. Peary followed a while later with Ooqueah and Egingwah.

A few hours into the march, Henson came close to losing his life. Forsaking caution, he stepped out onto thin ice covering a lead. His feet broke through the ice, and he sank up to his mouth in the frigid water. Ootah pulled Henson clear and helped to get him dried off and warm. Henson thanked his rescuer, telling him, "Ootah is very strong." The Eskimo re-plied sternly that he was not crazy like Henson. He knew better than to go out on thin ice.

They finally managed to cross the lead. Hours later, Henson stopped and backtracked a ways before making camp. He believed that he might have over-shot the Pole. Henson knew Peary would not be pleased to hear this because of a conversation they had earlier. Peary had told him to stop a little distance from the approximate position of the Pole. The com-mander had said, "I'll take one of the boys [Eskimos] and go on from there." Amazed, Henson had asked Peary whether or not he would be joining the com-mander. "I meant *we'll* take one of the boys," Peary

*Henson was responsible for breaking the trail on the final leg of the trek to the North Pole.*

*Henson (left) and an Eskimo assistant hold American flags as they celebrate the end of their quest for the Pole.*

responded. But Henson thought that Peary had let slip his real intentions: to have his black companion wait behind so that he could claim to have been the very first man at the North Pole.

When Peary arrived at the final camp, Henson was surprised to see that the commander showed no jubilation at reaching his destination. He said hardly a word to Henson and made no effort to congratulate his assistant. Despite the strain between the two men, they had achieved their goal. On the morning of April 7, Peary made one sighting with his sextant at the camp. He then drove off with two of the Eskimos to make more observations from different points in the area. Henson was left behind at the camp. When the commander returned, he announced that his sightings showed them to be on the approximate position of the North Pole.

Peary had Henson and the four Eskimos stand on a nearby pressure ridge while he photographed them. Henson stood in the middle with the American flag in his hands. The Eskimos held flags representing the U.S. Navy, the Red Cross, and other organizations that Peary wished to honor.

Henson said to Ootah, "We have found what we hunt."

Ootah looked at Henson strangely and then looked all around him. "There is nothing here. Just ice," he replied, and shrugged his shoulders.

There was little time to savor the triumph. Because the amount of daylight hours was increasing every day, the temperature might rise, causing unpassable leads to open up. They might soon become trapped hundreds of miles from land.

On April 7, Peary's small band of explorers began the journey back across the sea ice. As usual, Henson led the dash back to land. Peary rode on a sledge for most of the way. Even though this time they had plenty of supplies, Henson pushed the team very hard.

The lead that had delayed the men on the trek north was frozen solid, and on April 21, they crossed it and sped onward. Two days later they reached Cape Columbia. As soon as they stepped on land again, the Eskimos leaped up and down and laughed until they had to sink to the ground and gasp for breath. Henson laughed along with them, kidding them good-naturedly about their fear of the devil Tahnusuk. Ootah said the devil must have been asleep or having trouble with his wife to have let them come and go so easily.

After resting at the camp at Cape Columbia for two days, they marched eastward toward the *Roosevelt*. On April 25, they were greeted on the trail by Bartlett, who had returned to the ship a few days before. All the other members of the expedition had arrived back on land safely—except for Marvin. The Eskimos who had traveled back with Marvin said that he had fallen into a lead and drowned. Many years later, one of the Eskimos would confess that he had killed Marvin. The murderer claimed that he had been driven mad by the strain of traveling on the sea ice. In any event, the loss of Marvin cast a pall over the celebration on the ship.

Henson had toiled with remarkable energy, endurance, and courage to achieve his life's goal. He was 42 years old when he succeeded in traveling to the top of the world. Now he could rest, feeling that when he returned to the United States he would be widely honored as a national hero.

He was wrong. 

*The American flag rises high above a ridge at the North Pole. After taking latitude measurements on April 7, 1909, Peary announced that the team was standing on the top of the world.*

# 8

# A COOL
# RECEPTION

⟨⟨⟨⟩⟩⟩

THE EXPEDITION SAILED south from Cape Sheridan on July 18, 1909. Stopping at the Eskimo settlement at Etah, Peary heard some stunning news from an American who had spent the winter in Greenland. The man said that Dr. Frederick Cook, who had sailed with Peary and Henson in 1891, was claiming that he had reached the North Pole in April 1908.

Both Peary and Henson were instantly suspicious of Cook's claim. Neither of them believed that Cook possessed the skills needed to travel across 400 miles of polar-sea ice. Henson found the two Eskimos who had accompanied Cook on his trek. When questioned, they admitted that Cook had carried only a small amount of supplies. Furthermore, the men stated that they had never been out of sight of land. They had merely skirted the coast of Ellesmere Island.

As the *Roosevelt* steamed homeward, a great debate had already begun: Was Cook or Peary the true conqueror of the Pole? The American public sided overwhelmingly with Cook. Peary had a well-deserved reputation for arrogance, whereas Cook had an open, friendly manner that charmed people. When Peary asserted that Cook was a fraud, the doctor responded by saying that they had no reason to fight;

*The explorer Clyde Eddy watches as Henson signs the membership book of the Explorers Club in 1940. Most of the honors that Henson received came very late in his life.*

*In this 1909 cartoon, Great Britain's John Bull glowers and America's Uncle Sam celebrates as Robert Peary and Frederick Cook stake their separate claims to the North Pole.*

there was glory enough for both of them. The debate raged on for months, and many of Cook's supporters began to claim that Peary's expedition had not made it all the way to the Pole.

The brooding Peary retreated to his Maine home to prepare the records of his expedition. Neither of the two explorers was quick to produce the notebooks and diaries they had kept on their travels. Scientific organizations demanded to see the records of the measurements they had made on their expeditions. Cook said that he was planning to turn his records over to the Danish Geographic Society, an organization that specialized in arctic studies. In the meantime, he earned a great deal of money by writing and speaking about his explorations.

Henson soon became highly involved in the debate. After the *Roosevelt* docked in New York, he had a joyous reunion with his wife. Lucy quit her job, expecting that some organization would give her husband an important job that befitted his status as a famous explorer. But neither fame nor fortune came Henson's way. In fact, newspaper accounts about Peary's expedition hardly even mentioned Henson. Lucy returned to her job, and Henson began working as a garage attendant. However, a local promoter heard about Henson's arctic adventures and offered to send him on a lecture tour. Henson agreed, believing that it would be a good opportunity to earn some money and defend Peary's claims to the Pole.

From the time they had left the Pole, Peary had hardly spoken to Henson, and he did not approve of his black assistant's lecture tour. When Henson wrote to the commander asking for the loan of some photographs from the expedition, Peary refused, stating that he reserved the right to be the first one to talk and write about his expeditions.

Despite Peary's disapproval, Henson held his lecture tour, speaking in many cities across the United States. After an initial period of nervousness, he proved himself to be quite capable at public speaking. Yet he experienced constant harassment from Cook's supporters as well as from bigots in the audiences, and he finally had to end the tour.

Racism played a major role in the Peary-Cook debate. Peary's critics demanded to know why he had taken "an ignorant negro" instead of Bartlett with him on the last march to the Pole. The other team members defended Peary's decision to take the more experienced Henson, but the controversy persisted. Cook's supporters claimed that Henson had been chosen because he did not know how to make latitude measurements with a sextant and Peary could therefore deceive him about the team's true position. The critics said that Peary could not have fooled Bartlett. Amid the charges and countercharges and ugly racial arguments, the fact that Henson had unparalleled arctic experience and was a superb handler of dog teams was completely ignored.

*Frederick Cook, the doctor who accompanied Peary and Henson on the 1891–92 expedition, was unable to substantiate his claims to have reached the Pole in 1908.*

*Although Henson never returned to the Far North after 1909, he was long remembered by his Eskimo friends, who made his expression Ahdoolo a term for courage and perseverance.*

The response that Peary gave to defend his choice of Henson over Bartlett was shameful. He stated that he could not have let Henson take a group back by himself because, due to his racial background, he lacked the "initiative and daring" necessary for leading a team. This statement was clearly nonsense, but it fit in with the attitudes and perceptions of many prejudiced Americans. Many whites found it comforting to believe that blacks were incapable of major accomplishments. Henson was infuriated by Peary's statement, and the rift between them grew.

In January 1910, the Danish Geographic Society published its report on Cook's expedition. According to the society's findings, there was no evidence to show that Cook had traveled anywhere near the Pole. The records he submitted to prove his claims were found to be without any scientific value. Public opinion immediately turned against Cook, and Peary's claim to the Pole was recognized by the majority of international scientific organizations. Numerous honors were showered on Peary, and he was appointed to the rank of admiral in the navy.

However, many people remained unconvinced that Peary had reached the North Pole, partly because the commander refused to submit his records to the Danish Geographic Society for evaluation. He showed them instead to the National Geographic Society, an American organization, which quickly acclaimed him as the conqueror of the Pole. Still, some experts on arctic exploration questioned how Peary and Henson had been able to head straight for the Pole without making any directional measurements during their last, five-day leg.

Henson continued trying to win recognition for his own important place in the Peary expedition, but he had limited success. In 1912, he published an account of his adventures, *A Negro Explorer at the North Pole.* He did not discuss his strained relationship with Peary, nor did he describe in full detail just how important a role he had played in the commander's expeditions. He probably believed that no publisher would agree to publish the book if Henson claimed a large share of the glory for himself.

Seeking to restore his friendship with Peary, Henson sought the commander's help in getting the book published. Peary wrote a dry, complimentary foreword to the book in which he praised Henson's intelligence and persistence. Unfortunately, the book did not sell well, and Henson had to return to his job at a Brooklyn garage.

Henson took this turn in his fortunes more or less in stride. When a black politician named Charles Anderson told him that it was an outrage that he had to park cars for a living, he replied with wry humor: "There're no sledge teams for me to drive around here, Charley." In a more serious vein, he told Anderson he understood that most of America was not ready to honor a black man as a national hero. Anderson replied that he intended to use his influence to get a job for Henson in the U.S. government.

Anderson was true to his word. Several months later, an appointment came through to Henson for a job in the New York office of the U.S. Customs Bureau. He would start there as . . . a 46-year-old messenger boy.

With typical energy, Henson learned about the business of collecting duties on imported goods as well as all the other responsibilities of the Customs Bureau. After a while, he earned a promotion to clerk. When he retired in 1940, after 28 years of service in the government, he received a pension of $1,020 a year. Peary, who had died in 1920, had been given a huge pension when he retired from the navy. It was yet another reminder to Henson of how unequal the rewards were for the two men of different races who had shared so much in the Arctic.

During a 1926 interview, Henson points to a chart showing the route he took to the North Pole. In May of that year, the Norwegian explorer Roald Amundsen flew to the Pole in a dirigible.

*Lucy Henson stands in front of an exhibit at the American Museum of Natural History devoted to Peary and Henson's arctic adventures.*

As the decades passed, black organizations mounted campaigns to win national recognition for Henson. In 1926, 1936, 1938, and 1949, bills were presented in Congress asking that Henson be granted a pension for his work in the Arctic. Each of the bills was rejected. Forty years after the expedition to the North Pole, racist sentiments in Congress were still too strong for a measure to pass honoring Henson's achievements.

Donald MacMillan, who rose to the rank of admiral in the navy, fought valiantly on Henson's behalf. Gradually, a few honors were bestowed on Henson. In 1937, he was finally elected to the Explorers Club. In 1945, the navy honored all the members of Peary's polar expedition. Henson was presented with a medal by a young naval captain in the unadorned setting of an office room, where the sound of the typing pool continued during the ceremony. The officer read a statement praising Henson for his "fortitude, fearless determination, skillful performance . . . contributing materially to the success of the expedition in the discovery of the North Pole." The medal was made of silver and had a dramatic snow scene engraved on it. In the middle of the short ceremony, the young officer suddenly realized something: The Pole had been discovered 35 years before. He cleared his throat and said to the 79-year-old man who stood before him, "They sure took a long time to give you this."

Very late in his life, Henson finally received full national recognition for his accomplishments. In 1954, he and his wife, Lucy, were received at the White House by President Dwight D. Eisenhower. The two men stood together, looking down at the top of a globe and the small white splotch that represented the region in which Henson had spent his most exciting and productive years.

Henson died on March 9, 1955, when he was 88 years old. Black organizations in Maryland later persuaded the governor to declare April 6, 1959, as Matthew Henson Day. A bronze memorial plaque with Henson's face engraved on it was later installed in the Maryland state house.

Although Henson never returned to the Arctic after 1909, the Eskimos whom he had grown so close to carried on his name in many stories. Peter Freuchen, a Dane who lived among the Greenland Eskimos for many years, wrote, "It was not long before I became acquainted with the strange songs and fabulous legends relating the greatness of a man the natives called Miy Paluk. . . . To the Eskimos, who loved him, Matt was the greatest of all the men who came from the distant land of the south."

In 1987, S. Allen Counter, an authority on Henson's life, confirmed that Henson fathered a child in 1906 with an Eskimo woman—although he was never able to return to see his only child. However, Counter reports that to this day, Henson's descendants proudly relate their lineage from the mighty Miy Paluk.

A great sign of the respect and love the Eskimos had for Henson is the adoption of his word "Ahdoolo" into their language. Ahdoolo is a nonsense word that he invented and that he used early in the morning to rouse the Eskimos for a tough day on the trail. It always made them laugh to wake up to its un-Eskimo-sounding tones.

Over the years, the word has acquired a special meaning: It expresses readiness to summon up endurance and courage to face hard work and danger with hope and good spirits. Such traits were characteristic of Matthew Henson. His willingness to brave constantly changing hazards is not only the mark of a man well suited for adventure and exploration, but of a man who merits our admiration and respect. ✺

*Henson relaxes at his home in New York City. In 1954, President Dwight Eisenhower invited him to attend a ceremony in his honor at the White House.*

# CHRONOLOGY

| | |
|---|---|
| Aug. 8, 1866 | Born Matthew Henson in Charles County, Maryland |
| 1867 | Henson family sells farm and moves to Georgetown, on the outskirts of Washington, D.C. |
| 1879–1883 | Henson sails on the *Katie Hines* to ports in China, Japan, Africa, and the Russian Arctic seas |
| 1887 | Joins Robert Peary on an expedition to Nicaragua |
| 1891 | Henson makes his first voyage to Greenland with Peary, aboard the *Kite* |
| 1893–1895 | Henson's second trip to Greenland, aboard the *Falcon*; builds Anniversary Lodge and accompanies Peary on journey to northern Greenland |
| 1896–1897 | Henson and Peary sail on the *Hope* and recover a 35-ton portion of a meteorite |
| 1898 | Henson begins a four-year expedition with Peary in the Arctic |
| 1902 | Henson begins work as a Pullman porter, traveling across the country; becomes engaged to Lucy Ross |
| 1905–1906 | Accompanies Peary on expedition that travels to within 175 miles of the North Pole |
| 1907 | Marries Lucy Ross |
| July 6, 1908 | Expedition leaves New York to reach the North Pole |
| April 6, 1909 | Henson, Peary, and four Eskimos become the first men to reach the North Pole |
| 1912 | Henson publishes *A Negro Explorer at the North Pole* |
| 1913 | Begins work for the United States Customs Bureau |
| 1937 | Is elected to the Explorers Club |
| 1945 | Is awarded a medal from the navy |
| 1954 | Is invited to the White House |
| March 9, 1955 | Henson dies |

# FURTHER READING

Angell, Pauline K. *To the Top of the World.* New York: Rand McNally, 1964.

Dolan, Edward F. *Matthew Henson, Black Explorer.* New York: Dodd, Mead, 1979.

Henson, Matthew. *A Black Explorer at the North Pole.* New York: Walker, 1969.

Miller, Floyd. *Ahdoolo.* New York: E.P. Dutton, 1963.

Peary, Robert E. *The North Pole.* Mineola, NY: Dover Publications, 1986.

Peary, Robert E. *Northward Over the Great Ice.* New York: Frederick A. Stokes, 1898.

Robinson, Bradley with Matthew Henson. *Dark Companion.* New York: McBride and Co., 1947.

Weems, John Edward. *Race for the Pole.* New York: Henry Holt, 1960.

# INDEX

# PICTURE CREDITS

———— ❦ ————

MICHAEL GILMAN was born and educated in New York City. Along with writing, his interests include jogging and rock climbing. He and his wife, Nadine, have been married since 1982.

NATHAN IRVIN HUGGINS is W.E.B. Du Bois Professor of History and Director of the W.E.B. Du Bois Institute for Afro-American Research at Harvard University. He previously taught at Columbia University. Professor Huggins is the author of numerous books, including *Black Odyssey: The Afro-American Ordeal in Slavery, The Harlem Renaissance,* and *Slave and Citizen: The Life of Frederick Douglass.*